Teacher's Guide

Reading EXPLORER
2

Paul MacIntyre • Nancy Hubley

HEINLE
CENGAGE Learning™

Australia • Brazil • Japan • Korea • Mexico • Singapore • Spain • United Kingdom • United States

HEINLE
CENGAGE Learning™

Reading Explorer Teacher's Guide 2
Paul MacIntyre and Nancy Hubley

VP and Director of Operations:
Vincent Grosso

Publisher: Andrew Robinson

Executive Editor: Sean Bermingham

Senior Development Editor: Derek Mackrell

Assistant Editor: Sarah Tan

Director of Global Marketing: Ian Martin

Director of US Marketing: Jim McDonough

Content Project Manager: Tan Jin Hock

Senior Print Buyer: Mary Beth Hennebury

National Geographic Coordinator:
Leila Hishmeh

Contributing Editor: Joan Ho

Cover Designer: Page 2, LLC

Compositor: Pre-PressPMG

Acknowledgments
The Author and Publishers would like to thank
the following teaching professionals for their
valuable feedback during the development of
this series.

Jamie Ahn, English Coach, Seoul;
Heidi Bundschoks, ITESM, Sinaloa México;
José Olavo de Amorim, Colégio Bandeirantes,
São Paulo; **Marina Gonzalez**, Instituto
Universitario de Lenguas Modernas Pte.,
Buenos Aires; **Tsung-Yuan Hsiao**, National
Taiwan Ocean University, Keelung; **Michael
Johnson**, Muroran Institute of Technology;
Thays Ladosky, Colégio Damas, Recife; **Ahmed
Mohamed Motala**, University of Sharjah;
David Persey, British Council, Bangkok;
David Schneer, ACS International, Singapore;
Atsuko Takase, Kinki University, Osaka;
Deborah E. Wilson, American University
of Sharjah

This series is dedicated to the memory of Joe
Dougherty, who was a constant inspiration
throughout its development.

ISBN-13: 978-1-4240-2940-2

ISBN-10: 1-4240-2940-6

US edition ISBN-13: 978-1-4240-4550-1

US edition ISBN-10: 1-4240-4550-9

Heinle
20 Channel Center Street
Boston, Massachusetts 02210
USA

Cengage Learning is a leading provider of customized learning solutions with
office locations around the globe, including Singapore, the United Kingdom,
Australia, Mexico, Brazil, and Japan. Locate our local office at:
international.cengage.com/region

Cengage Learning products are represented in Canada by
Nelson Education, Ltd.

Visit Heinle online at **elt.heinle.com**

Visit our corporate website at **www.cengage.com**

Printed in the United States of America
1 2 3 4 5 6 7 – 13 12 11 10 09

Contents

Take a Tour of *Reading Explorer* 4

Unit Walkthrough 6

Aims and Principles of *Reading Explorer* 8

Preparing Learners to Read 9

Building Learners' Reading Skills 10

Developing Learners' Vocabulary 12

Developing Visual Literacy 15

Using Video in Class 19

Exploring Further: Reading and Viewing 20

Assessing Learners' Progress 21

Teaching Notes

Unit 1: On the Menu 22

Unit 2: Animals and Language 26

Unit 3: History Detectives 30

Review 1: Buried Cities 34

A Global View: Languages 35

Unit 4: Great Destinations 38

Unit 5: Storms 42

Unit 6: Reef Encounters 46

Review 2: Underwater Wonders 50

A Global View: Water 51

Unit 7: Sweet Scents 54

Unit 8: Great Explorers 58

Unit 9: Traditions and Rituals 62

Review 3: Cities of Gold and Mud 66

A Global View: Trade 67

Unit 10: Global Warming 70

Unit 11: Incredible Insects 74

Unit 12: Going to Extremes 78

Review 4: The Grand Canyon 82

A Global View: Climate 83

Photocopiable Worksheets 86

Target Vocabulary Definitions 90

Glossary of Terms 95

Recommended Graded Readers 96

Take a Tour of *Reading Explorer*

Thank you for choosing to use Reading Explorer Book 2. Here are 12 steps to help you get familiar with the course:

1. First, look at the list of **Contents** on page 3 of the Student Book. You'll see the book is organized into 12 units and 4 review sections. The book can be used for a short course of 24–36 hours using just the core units or can be extended for longer courses, for example, by using the video activities and review units in class.

2. Turn to the world map on pages 4–5 of the Student Book, under the title **Explore Your World!** The photographs and captions highlight some of the topics and places that are explored in the book. Have learners follow the page references as a way to get them into the book at the start of the first lesson.

3. Look at the **Scope and Sequence** on pages 6–7 of the Student Book. You'll see that each unit is based on a theme of general interest, for example, "Animals and Language." Within each unit are two lessons, each based around a reading passage. You'll also note the range of vocabulary building skills covered in the book.

4. Read the **Introduction** on page 8 of the Student Book. It explains a general approach to developing reading skills commonly known as *KWL*. The aim of this approach—and of this course, in general—is to develop active, fluent readers. For more on teaching reading skills, see pages 8–12 of this Teacher's Guide.

5. Skim through a **Unit** of the Student Book and compare it against the Unit Walkthrough on the following pages of this Teacher's Guide. Each unit is accompanied in the Teacher's Guide by teaching suggestions and background notes (see pages 22–85).

6. Turn to one of the **Reading Passages** in the Student Book (e.g., Student Book page 11). The reading passages are all adapted from authentic National Geographic sources, which are listed in the **Credits** on pages 191–192 of the Student Book. Each reading passage is also available as an audio recording on the **Classroom Audio CD** as well as on the **Student CD-ROM**, providing a useful model for pronunciation and intonation.

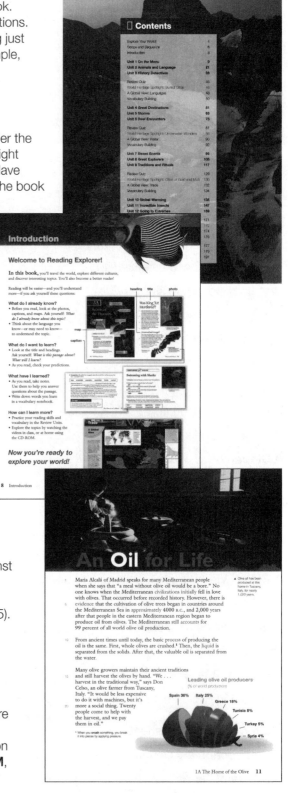

7. You'll note in each reading passage that useful, high-frequency words are highlighted in red. These **Target Vocabulary** words are listed on pages 177–178 of the Student Book, and also, with definitions, at the back of this Teacher's Guide (pages 90–94). For suggestions on teaching vocabulary, see pages 12–14 of this Teacher's Guide.

8. Check out the **Video clips** on the Video DVD and Student CD-ROM. The clips can be used with the **Explore More** section at the end of each Student Book unit, and also with the video comprehension activities on the Student CD-ROM. The scripts for the videos are on pages 179–190 of the Student Book. You'll see that the video narration recycles many of the target vocabulary items. For ideas on using video in class, see pages 19–20 of this Teacher's Guide.

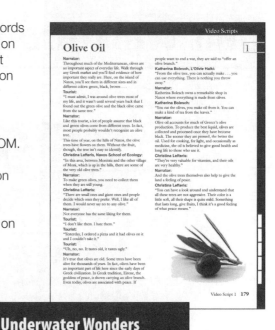

9. After each set of three units is a **Review** section (e.g., Student Book pages 45–50). Included in this section is a two-page **World Heritage Spotlight**, preceded by a **Field Notes** task. There is also a section (**A Global View**) that focuses on an important global issue. Suggestions for presenting these in class are provided in this Teacher's Guide (e.g., pages 34–37). The review units tie in with National Geographic Society's efforts to raise awareness of heritage and conservation.

10. Check out the range of ancillary components of the course. The **Student CD-ROM** contains the 12 video clips, audio recordings of the 24 reading passages, and a variety of interactive comprehension and vocabulary activities. The activities are self-grading and provide reinforcement for the language presented in each unit. Additional learning and teaching resources are available online at elt.heinle.com/explorer.

11. An **Assessment CD-ROM** containing Exam*View*® question banks is available for teachers who want to create customized tests or give students additional language practice. See page 21 of this Teacher's Guide for suggestions on assessing learners' progress.

12. Finally, turn to the back page of this Teacher's Guide, and you'll see a list of **recommended graded readers** from the Heinle *Footprint Reading Library*, a range of nonfiction readers based on video content from National Geographic, and correlated with CEF (Common European Framework) levels. Extensive reading for pleasure is a proven way to promote reading proficiency. See elt.heinle.com/ng for the full range of leveled readers, audio, and video components.

Unit Walkthrough

Warm Up discussion questions help to raise learners' interest in the unit theme and activate learners' prior knowledge.

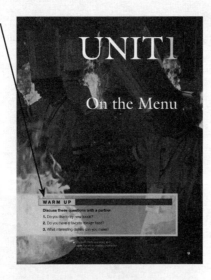

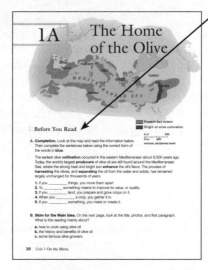

Before You Read tasks introduce key terms and content that learners will encounter in the reading passage, and develop previewing skills such as skimming and making predictions.

Each **Reading Passage** is adapted from an authentic *National Geographic* source; the language has been carefully graded and the reading contains ten high-frequency "target vocabulary" items.

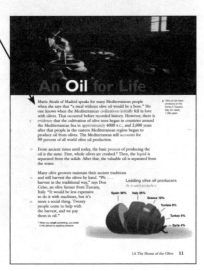

Photographs and graphics from *National Geographic* provide rich context for the reading topics.

Reading Comprehension tasks include a variety of graphic organizers, which help learners to understand the relationship between key ideas in the passage.

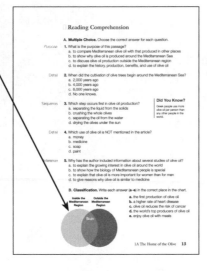

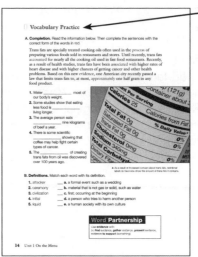

Vocabulary Practice activities reinforce the acquisition of "target vocabulary" items presented in the main passage.

Real-life materials such as menus relate topics to students' everyday experiences.

A second reading in each unit expands learners' knowledge of the unit theme and further builds vocabulary.

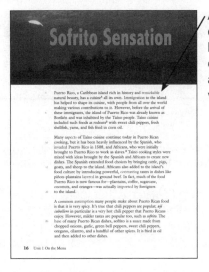

Photo captions, charts, and graphs develop learners' visual literacy—their ability to decode graphic information effectively.

Reading Comprehension activities include question types commonly found in high-stakes international exams, such as TOEFL® and TOEIC®.

Vocabulary Builder boxes highlight common collocations, affixes, and usage to develop learner independence.

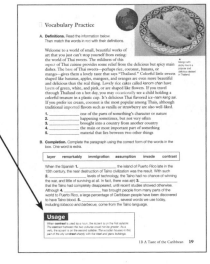

Explore More video activities provide additional comprehension and vocabulary practice while motivating learners to learn more about the unit topic.

Further comprehension and vocabulary practice is provided on the Student CD-ROM, which contains all 12 video clips, audio recordings of the 24 reading passages, and more than 80 self-scoring activities.

Aims and Principles of *Reading Explorer*

The *Reading Explorer* series aims to develop learners' skills in reading, vocabulary building, and critical thinking, using topics and visuals adapted from real-world National Geographic content.

A key principle of *Reading Explorer* is that today's learners need to be exposed to a wide variety of reading types. Information in the twenty-first century is increasingly conveyed in **multimodal** formats, that is, using a combination of text with graphics, diagrams, tables, photographs, and video. Exposure to the variety of formats in *Reading Explorer* will help learners to develop their visual literacy as well as textual literacy.

Another principle of *Reading Explorer* is that fluent readers employ a variety of strategies for reading, which, in turn, is based on various purposes for reading. In other words, the reading process is often **multipurpose**.

With *Reading Explorer*, learners develop strategies such as:

- Using their own background knowledge of the topic, and awareness of text types, in order to make predictions about a passage;
- Reading "top-down" to gain an overall idea of the purpose, type, and structure of a text;
- Processing "bottom-up" clues such as contextual information and word parts in order to comprehend unfamiliar vocabulary, and the meaning of cohesive markers such as pronoun references;
- Scanning a text quickly to locate specific information;
- Processing what is literally given in a text (literal comprehension) as well as what is implied or inferred by the writer (inferential comprehension);
- Recognizing relationships within a paragraph, or across a text, such as identifying cause and effect relationships, or the links between main and supporting ideas;
- Identifying what is factually true in a text, versus the writer's personal opinion.

An additional principle of the series is that reading is a **multistage** process. In particular, learners should be well prepared before they start to read a text and should later have an opportunity to reflect on what they have learned. This concept is summarized in the **Introduction** on page 8 of the Student Book that outlines a framework known as the *KWL technique*.

Using this approach, students identify:

- What they *know* about the topic (i.e., their prior knowledge, or *schema*)
- What they *want* to know (i.e., their purpose for reading)
- What they *learned* (i.e., their comprehension of the reading)

With *Reading Explorer*, learners are also encouraged to go beyond the passage—and develop learner independence—by exploring the topic using the DVD, the Student CD-ROM, and the review units, as well as by exploring the topics online.

Preparing Learners to Read

How should teachers prepare for a unit?

Teachers should go through the unit themselves before a class, making note of any questions students may have. The Teacher's Guide provides background information and resources to help deal with students' questions. Relevant websites provide opportunities to learn more, and students can be directed to them for further exploration. Take time to read the overview, answer keys, and detailed teaching notes on language, cultural background, and vocabulary. The **Explore More** section gives teaching suggestions on using the video effectively.

Why is it important to prepare learners before reading?

Reading is an interaction between what students already know about a topic and new material in a reading passage. They will understand and enjoy reading more if their background knowledge is drawn upon. Moreover, learners need a *reason* to read.

How should teachers use the *Warm Up* section?

Every *Reading Explorer* unit starts with a section called **Warm Up**. This helps students make connections between what they already *know*—the "K" part of the KWL approach—and the topics covered in the unit. Full-page photographs from National Geographic help students to raise interest in the unit theme, and discussion questions help students relate the reading topics to their own lives. The Teacher's Guide provides possible responses to these questions as well as additional questions that encourage students to think about the overall theme of the unit.

How should teachers use the *Before You Read* section?

Before You Read is made up of two tasks, A and B, and comes at the start of each lesson. Task A pre-teaches some key vocabulary and content that is essential to understanding the reading passage. These words (i.e., the support vocabulary) are presented in context and set in blue for emphasis. This support vocabulary appears later in the passage and is important for overall comprehension; however, it is not essential that students acquire (i.e., learn and remember) these words at this stage. More explanation about vocabulary, including the distinction between support and target vocabulary, is given on pages 12–14.

In Task A, learners complete tasks such as using the blue words to label a photograph or map, matching definitions, answering questions, or completing a short paragraph. In the process, they build visual literacy skills by reading graphically presented information, such as captions, headers, map or graph keys, just as in magazines, in newspapers, or on the Internet.

Task B provides a purpose for reading. For example, students should read the reading passage quickly to identify the main idea or make predictions about the content. Establishing what they *want* to learn is the "W" in KWL. It is important that *after* reading, teachers should take time to see what students have *learned*—"L" in KWL—from the passage.

What are the main previewing skills?

The main previewing skills are *skimming* (reading quickly for the main idea), *scanning* (reading quickly to find specific information), and *predicting* (using existing knowledge of a topic to anticipate the content of the passage). By reading quickly first, students are motivated to read more thoroughly later.

Building Learners' Reading Skills

What are the features of *Reading Explorer* texts?

Target vocabulary items are highlighted in red within the passage. They are also listed at the back of the Student Book (pages 177–178 and defined on pages 90–94 of this Teacher's Guide). These high-frequency words have been selected because they occur often in nonfiction reading. They are the useful words that students should learn and remember. Target vocabulary is developed further in the vocabulary section within each unit and recycled throughout the series.

Teachers can teach target vocabulary in various ways. Some teachers may prefer to pre-teach these words before learners read the passage; others may prefer to wait until after learners have completed a first reading of the text, before they teach or elicit the meaning of the target words.

Line numbers are provided every five lines in each reading passage. In class discussions, encourage students to use the line numbers when responding to comprehension questions. When students work in pairs, ask them to refer to the text using line numbers.

Titles and headers provide clues to the organization of a reading passage and the main ideas. Sometimes the pre-reading activities will draw special attention to them. Ask students about titles and headers after a first reading. Check whether they are able to put the headers into their own words. Typically, each paragraph has one main idea expressed in the header.

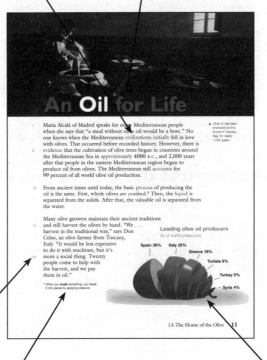

Footnote definitions for lower-frequency words (e.g., acronyms or technical terms) that are important for understanding the passage are provided at the bottom of the page.

Illustrations, maps, and captions provide information that reinforces or expands on ideas from the reading passage. If students haven't been directed to use these resources in **Before You Read**, draw attention to them by asking questions that can be answered only with information found there. The Teacher's Guide provides suggestions for utilizing these resources to help promote visual literacy.

How can teachers promote reading fluency?

Reading fluency is the ability to read smoothly and effortlessly while understanding the ideas expressed in the text. To help learners achieve this goal, teachers can:

- Encourage learners to read chunks of text by phrases, rather than word by word.
- Discourage learners from "tracing" words with their fingers—or subvocalizing (reading aloud) the words while reading—as it slows down the reading process.
- In subsequent readings of the passage, have students read quickly without stopping for a timed period such as two minutes. Then check how far the learners get each time.
- Play the audio recording of the passage from the CD, and have learners read the passage at the same speed.
- Recommend that learners avoid checking each unfamiliar word in a dictionary, particularly when they read a passage for the first time.

How should teachers check reading comprehension?

Reading comprehension activities check students' understanding and their ability to use specific reading skills. The comprehension section immediately follows each reading passage. Some teachers may prefer to have students attempt to answer the questions without referring back to the text. However, note that some questions in Part A specifically refer to paragraphs or lines in the text.

How does *Reading Explorer* prepare students for standardized tests?

Reading Explorer has texts and question types similar to those used on international English exams. The labels on the questions are an effective teaching tool to familiarize students with their purposes and formats. The labels are explained in the glossary at the end of the Teacher's Guide.

Task A:

This task has five multiple-choice questions. Each one focuses on one of the following skills:

- Understanding the gist (overall theme) of the entire passage
- Choosing the main idea or the most appropriate title for the passage
- Identifying the main idea of smaller portions of text (e.g., a paragraph)
- Finding factual details (usually paraphrased from the text)
- Identifying the meaning of references in the text, e.g. pronoun references
- Understanding the meaning of vocabulary in context (different from target or support vocabulary)
- Paraphrasing ideas
- Inferring someone's intention or opinion
- Detecting the author's purpose
- Checking the accuracy of statements

Task B:

This section consists of a comprehension task that checks students' understanding of relationships between different parts of the text. Typical Part B tasks include:

- Categorizing concepts with Venn diagrams (e.g., page 13 of the Student Book)
- Sequencing information (e.g., page 67 of the Student Book)
- Understanding steps in a process (e.g., page 139 of the Student Book)
- Matching key information (e.g., page 168 of the Student Book)

- Understanding cause and effect (e.g., page 72 of the Student Book)
- Matching main ideas or headings with paragraphs (e.g., page 102 of the Student Book)
- Completing summaries with key words (e.g., page 55 of the Student Book)
- Recognizing true or false statements (e.g., page 18 of the Student Book)
- Differentiating fact from opinion (e.g., page 42 of the Student Book)

The use of several types of graphic organizers in Task B (Venn diagrams, flow charts, time lines, etc.) helps to further develop learners' visual literacy skills. (See also pages 15–18 of this Teacher's Guide.)

Additional reading comprehension questions can be found on the Student Book CD-ROM.

The worksheet on page 86 of this Teacher's Guide may be photocopied and given to students to complete in class, either while they read or after they have finished the reading and the comprehension task.

For further ideas on developing reading skills and fluency, see Anderson, N. J. (1999). *Exploring Second Language Reading: Issues and Strategies*. Boston: Heinle and the online professional training courses available at eltadvantage. heinle.com.

Developing Learners' Vocabulary

What is *Reading Explorer's* approach to language learning?

Reading Explorer aims to build the high-frequency vocabulary that learners need for academic and real-world success. The series presents words in context, and then follows with exercises that teach and recycle them. Vocabulary research has shown that both implicit and explicit instruction are important in developing vocabulary that students can retain and actively use. *Reading Explorer* provides teachers with both options.

What are the different types of vocabulary in *Reading Explorer*?

All components of *National Geographic Reading Explorer*—reading texts, video, and audio—are carefully graded to build students' vocabulary. *Reading Explorer* categorizes vocabulary into the following types:

- *Target vocabulary*: These are high-frequency words in academic and non-fiction reading. Knowing them and their related forms will help students become effective and fluent readers. Target words are highlighted in red. Target vocabulary is practiced in the **Vocabulary Practice** section of each unit of the Student Book (e.g., page 14), in the review units, and on the CD-ROM.
- *Support vocabulary*: These words appear in blue in each unit's **Before You Read** section and are accompanied by photographs and graphics that help learners understand their meaning. They pre-teach vocabulary related to the topic of the reading passage.
- *Specialized or technical vocabulary*: These are footnoted within each passage, with definitions provided beneath the text.

What are some ways to teach vocabulary in context?

When learning another language, students need specific instructions in order to build vocabulary rapidly. Guessing the meaning of unknown or new words from context works best when students have already developed a sizeable core vocabulary. For this reason, teachers may choose to pre-teach the target vocabulary before learners approach the reading. Definitions of **Target Vocabulary** are provided on pages 90–94 of this Teacher's Guide; these definitions are based on the use of the words within the reading passages.

However, even elementary and intermediate students benefit from being taught skills for understanding new vocabulary in context. Here are some suggestions for building these skills:

- Draw attention to the target vocabulary highlighted in the passage. Have students pay attention to the surrounding words. Is the new word associated or collocated with other words?
- Decide on the new word's part of speech. How does it function in the sentence? Are there clues such as articles (*an*, *the*), adjectives, adverbs, or verb endings?
- Are some components of the word familiar? Look for clues to meaning in word roots, prefixes, and suffixes.
- Is the new word defined within the text? Sometimes a synonym is given nearby in the passage.

Teaching strategies for understanding words from context will promote better reading skills. Whenever possible, encourage students to work out meaning from context without interrupting the flow of their reading. In particular, suggest that students avoid using a dictionary to look up word meanings while reading, as this will slow them down and decrease their reading fluency.

The Teacher's Guide contains suggestions for presenting and practicing vocabulary for each unit. In addition, clarifications are provided for appropriate usage and cultural considerations of certain words.

How is target vocabulary practiced and reviewed?

After being presented in context in the main reading passage, target vocabulary items are subsequently recycled in several sections of the book:

1. The **Vocabulary Practice** page in each unit focuses on using the target vocabulary in various contexts. Sometimes students complete gaps in a reading with the key words. At other times, they manipulate target words or find appropriate definitions for them in context.

   Knowing a word does not just involve knowing its spelling and meaning; it is also important that learners become aware of word structure, collocations, and usage. While much of the focus of the **Vocabulary Practice** page is on word meaning, the **Vocabulary Builder** boxes supplement this by highlighting relevant word forms and associations. There are three types in Student Book 2:

   Word Link: Students develop decoding strategies based on word parts such as roots, prefixes, and suffixes.

   Word Partnerships: Common collocations and set phrases involving target vocabulary items are presented, so that learners can increase their vocabulary awareness through acquisition of lexical chunks.

   Usage: Information is provided on common usage, such as the varied meanings of a word, and the distinction between formal and slang connotations.

   Thesaurus: Common synonyms are provided for key words.

2. The **Explore More** section in each unit is based on a short video on a topic related to the unit theme. The video is included on both the classroom DVD and Student CD-ROM. Many of the target vocabulary items are featured on the narration of the video which has been carefully graded for language level. A summary cloze activity (Task B) recycles target vocabulary from both lessons of the unit. **Think About It** questions then give students an opportunity to use newly acquired vocabulary as they discuss the unit topic and relate it to their own lives.

   For more on using video in class, see pages 19–20 of this Teacher's Guide.

3. The **Review Unit** provides additional practice with target vocabulary.

   Each review unit starts with a crossword puzzle featuring words from the three previous units. The puzzle checks students' understanding of meanings and definitions as well as accuracy of spelling. Students can prepare for this by referring to the **Target Vocabulary** index on pages 177–178 of the Student Book. This list is cross-referenced with units and lessons. In addition, a target vocabulary list with definitions is provided on pages 90–94 of this Teacher's Guide.

The review unit continues with the completion of **Field Notes**—similar to brief notes that a researcher might make when visiting a World Heritage Site. The notes, which recycle many of the target vocabulary items from previous units, provide a model for taking notes on key information. The task relates to the following double-page **World Heritage Spotlight** section, which recycles several target vocabulary items in new contexts.

Target vocabulary is again recycled in the **Global View** pages of each Review. This section provides a graphic overview of an important global issue, and further helps to develop learners' critical thinking and visual literacy skills (see pages 15–18 of this Teacher's Guide).

The last page of the review unit focuses on **Vocabulary Building** and consists of two sections. **Task A** reviews words and phrases highlighted in the preceding Global View spread; students use the words to complete definitions or a paragraph. **Task B** reviews and gives further examples of word forms described in previous units. For example, the **Word Link** section might cover suffixes such as *–tion* and *–sion* that change verbs into nouns. Students focus on individual words, then use them to complete a reading passage.

4. Additional vocabulary practice exercises can be found on the **Student CD-ROM**. These interactive and self-scoring activities review the target vocabulary from the Student Book and include question types such as multiple-choice, drag and drop, and sentence completion.

What role do dictionaries play in learning?

Although target vocabulary is presented and practiced in context in *Reading Explorer*, dictionaries still play an important role in learning vocabulary. Whichever dictionary you and your students decide to use, it is important to become familiar with its features and use it regularly. Some teachers find it helpful to bring a range of dictionaries to class and develop activities that require students to contrast and compare them.

The **Vocabulary Builder** boxes found on the vocabulary practice page of the Student Book are closely based on similar features found in the Collins COBUILD range of American English dictionaries. These dictionaries are based on an extensive corpus of real-world examples and include full-sentence definitions as well as information on word origins, collocations, and usage. For more information on Collins COBUILD dictionaries, visit elt.heinle.com.

What tips can teachers offer students in learning vocabulary?

As a teacher, you can help learners become successful language learners by:

- Creating opportunities for vocabulary practice and making it fun
- Making your classroom "vocabulary rich" by placing notes and labels on walls and boards
- Creating flashcards and games (such as bingo and "hangman") as a way of reviewing recently learned vocabulary
- Including vocabulary in your assessment
- Teaching vocabulary acquisition strategies (such as learning key affixes and word roots)
- Using word webs, drawings, and other memory aids to help students remember words
- Requiring students to keep vocabulary notebooks and checking them often
- Promoting extensive reading by encouraging learners to read graded readers, such as the *Footprint Reading Library* titles listed in the list of **Recommended Graded Readers** on page 96 of this Teacher's Guide.

For further ideas on teaching vocabulary, see Nation, I. S. P. (2008). *Teaching Vocabulary: Strategies and Techniques*. Boston: Heinle and the online professional training courses available at eltadvantage.heinle.com.

Developing Visual Literacy

Over the last few decades, the uses and forms of writing have undergone profound changes. For today's students, linear written text is no longer the only (or, in some cases, even the main) form of representing information.

In a recent U.S.-based study of print and online learning resources in English, Science, and Mathematics, researchers identified two major trends (Bezemer and Kress, 2008):

1. Digital media (video, computers, etc.) are increasingly being used to distribute and present learning resources.
2. Writing is being displaced by image as the central mode for representation. In other words, textual information is being supplemented—and sometimes replaced—by other forms of visual representation, such as graphs, charts, pictures, and diagrams.

To address the first trend, the growing importance of **digital literacy**, the *Reading Explorer* series incorporates video tasks in each unit and encourages learners to go beyond the textbook by exploring topics online or using the Student CD-ROM. Teaching suggestions for these resources are provided on pages 19–21.

The development of learners' **visual literacy** (sometimes called *graphic literacy*) also plays a central role in *Reading Explorer.*

How is visual literacy developed in *Reading Explorer*?

Some graphic formats are called *graphic organizers* because they help readers organize information clearly in a visual way. Graphic organizers feature regularly in the **Reading Comprehension** exercises. These help students understand how ideas from the **Reading Passage** are related to one another.

Examples of graphic organizers include:

- Venn diagrams
- timelines
- flowcharts
- summary charts

Other graphic formats featured in the series—particularly in the **Global View** sections in each Review—include:

- maps
- bar graphs
- line graphs
- process diagrams

The following pages provide a visual overview of the types of graphic formats featured in *Reading Explorer*. These pages may be photocopied and handed out to students at the start of the course.

Teaching suggestions relating to each type are included on page 18.

Reference: Bezemer, J. and Kress, G. (2008). Writing in Multimodal Texts *Written Communication*, *25:2*, 166–195.

Reading Maps, Graphs, and Diagrams

As well as understanding written texts, fluent readers also need to be able to understand and use various types of graphs, maps, and diagrams. Here are some examples you will see in *Reading Explorer*.

Venn diagrams compare the characteristics of two or more categories.

Timelines show a sequence of events across time.

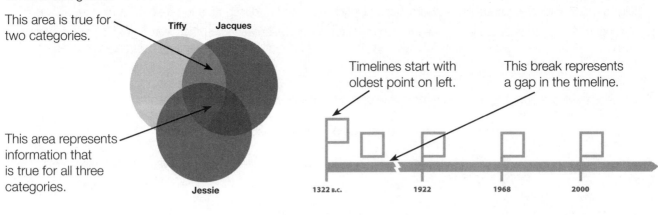

This area is true for two categories.

This area represents information that is true for all three categories.

Timelines start with oldest point on left.

This break represents a gap in the timeline.

Bar and line graphs use axes to show the relationship between two or more things. **Bar graphs** are useful for showing the values of various categories. **Line graphs** are often used to show how something rises and falls over time.

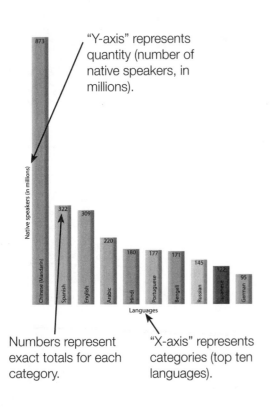

"Y-axis" represents quantity (number of native speakers, in millions).

Numbers represent exact totals for each category.

"X-axis" represents categories (top ten languages).

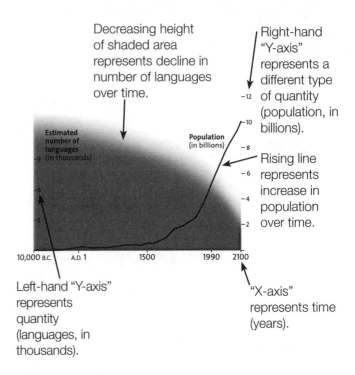

Decreasing height of shaded area represents decline in number of languages over time.

Right-hand "Y-axis" represents a different type of quantity (population, in billions).

Rising line represents increase in population over time.

Left-hand "Y-axis" represents quantity (languages, in thousands).

"X-axis" represents time (years).

A **pie chart** shows how something is made of various parts.

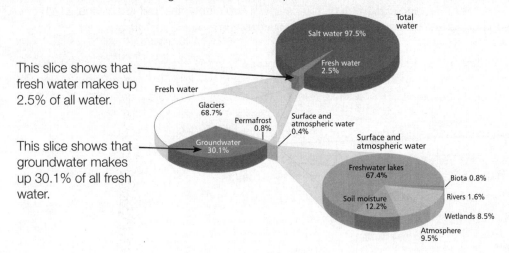

This slice shows that fresh water makes up 2.5% of all water.

This slice shows that groundwater makes up 30.1% of all fresh water.

Diagrams are a useful way to show how a process or system works.

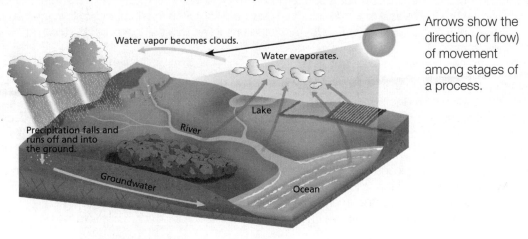

Arrows show the direction (or flow) of movement among stages of a process.

Maps are used to show geographic features.

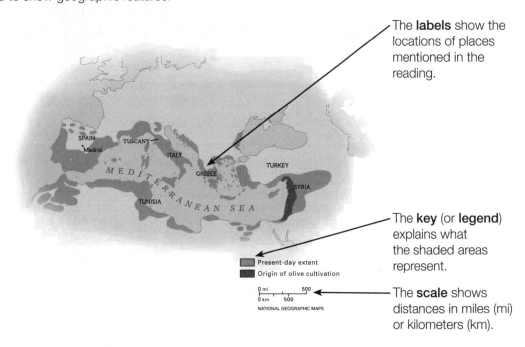

The **labels** show the locations of places mentioned in the reading.

The **key** (or **legend**) explains what the shaded areas represent.

The **scale** shows distances in miles (mi) or kilometers (km).

Venn Diagrams use overlapping circles to show the extent to which different categories share the same characteristics. Venn diagrams in *Reading Explorer* typically deal with two categories, but occasionally with three. Information that relates to both or all categories appears in the overlapping area.

Timelines organize information in sequence over a period of time, usually from far left (oldest) to far right (newest). Reference points are not always evenly spaced, so learners must understand the key and/or time labels. When needed, point out the historical division between B.C. (sometimes referred to as B.C.E., or "Before Common Era") and A.D.

Maps usually have the same basic features that should be pointed out to students:

- A *key* or *legend* uses symbols that tell what is represented.
- A *scale* shows how distances are represented in miles or kilometers.
- *Labels* identify physical features like oceans and political features like cities.
- *Compass points* show directions (N-E-S-W).
- *Lines (grid)* show the equator, longitude, and latitude.
- *Colors* may show different elevations of land.

Bar Graphs compare two or more categories such as countries or kinds of animals. The *horizontal* or *X-axis* usually shows the categories, while the *vertical* or *Y-axis* usually shows quantity. Often the number labels in the Y-axis represent larger values (for example, 1 = 1,000 or 1,000,000). Ask students to explain the labels before they do a reading task that involves using a chart.

Line Graphs are particularly useful in showing change through time. The *horizontal* or *X-axis* usually shows time increasing from left to right, while the *vertical* or *Y-axis* usually shows quantity. Trace the line from left to right to follow changes in quantity through time. Review vocabulary for trends such as *increasing*, *decreasing*, *stable*, *decline*, and so on, so students can interpret information on the graph.

Pie Charts look like pies cut into pieces and compare parts to wholes. For example, if the total population of language students is the whole, the sizes of the "slices" and their numerical values indicate how many students study each language. It may be useful to review with learners how to convert percentages to fractions and *vice versa*, in order for them to interpret and discuss information in a pie chart.

Diagrams and Flowcharts can represent simple or complex dynamic processes. Read labels carefully to select the best place to begin explaining the process, then take the students through it one step at a time. Ask them to describe how each step relates to preceding and following steps. A flowchart is a form of diagram that uses a series of text boxes that represent stages in a process.

Locator globes in each unit put the location of the reading or video in context.

Teacher notes provide more advice on interpreting specific graphics in each unit.

Using Video in Class

What are the features of the *Explore More* section?

Explore More features a video on a theme related to the whole unit. It has three tasks:

- *Preview:* This section prepares students for what they will be watching.
- *Summarize:* This section requires students to complete a cloze passage that summarizes what they have watched. It recycles target vocabulary and tests students' understanding of the video.
- *Think About It*: The questions in this section allow students to think critically about what they have learned in the unit, including ideas from the video, and to relate the unit to their own lives.

All video clips are on the Student CD-ROM as well as the classroom DVD. (Note that the classroom DVD is meant for use on a regular DVD player; the video clips on the CD-ROM are for use on a computer.) The Student CD-ROM also contains additional comprehension questions about the video.

Why teach video-viewing skills?

In daily life, nonfiction videos can be found on television, on the Internet, and in theaters as documentaries. Just as *Reading Explorer* provides a wide variety of authentic text and graphic material to build students' nonfiction reading skills, the series also builds viewing skills with videos from National Geographic. *Reading Explorer* promotes visual and digital literacy so learners can competently use a wide range of modern media.

Videos differ from word texts in important ways. First, students are processing information by viewing and listening simultaneously. Visual images include information about the video's setting as well as nonverbal communication such as facial expressions and body movements. The video may also include animated maps and diagrams to explain information and processes. The soundtrack contains narration, conversations, music, and sound effects. Some contextual words may appear on screen in signs or as identification of people or settings. In addition, full English subtitles ("closed captions") are available as a teaching and learning option.

What are the stages of viewing?

Previewing prepares students for the video, engages their background knowledge about the topic, and creates interest in what they will watch. Effective ways of previewing include:

- Brainstorming and discussing about what the class already knows about the topic
- Using photographs and the video's title to predict the content
- Pre-teaching key vocabulary essential to understanding the video content
- Skimming the summary reading

Viewing may occur multiple times and at different speeds while:

- Watching for gist comprehension or the main ideas from the film
- Watching and listening closely for detail
- Watching and listening for opinion and inference

Post-viewing activities include:

- Describing the main points and the sequence of events in the video
- Completing the cloze summary with provided target vocabulary
- Answering **Think About It** questions that relate the video to the students' own lives or experiences

How should teachers use the videos to teach?

The narration on each video has been carefully graded to feature vocabulary and structures that are appropriate for students' proficiency level. The location of the video section at the end of each unit ensures that students already bring background knowledge and target vocabulary to the viewing process.

Here are techniques for using video in class:

- Have students preview the video by reading the transcript or the summary paragraph.
- Pause, rewind, or fast-forward the video to focus on key segments or events.
- Pause the video midway to allow students to predict what will happen next. Resume the video so students can check their predictions.
- Have students watch the video with the sound muted, to focus only on what they see. If this approach is used, follow-up discussion helps students share their ideas about the content of the video. Then play with sound for students to check their ideas.
- Have students watch without subtitles after which they discuss what they heard; then play with subtitles for students to check their ideas.
- Have students follow the script as they listen to the video to help in improving intonation, pitch, and stress. Stop and replay key phrases for students to repeat.
- Have students watch the video independently and complete the comprehension questions on the Student CD-ROM.

Note that the cloze summary (Task B of **Explore More**) can be used without the video if desired. All video scripts are printed on pages 179–190 of the Student Book. Teachers have flexibility in how or whether they want students to use the scripts. See individual units in this Teacher's Guide for specific teaching suggestions for each video.

To extend viewing skills to speaking and writing skills, have students make a presentation or create a written report, about a short video of their choice, using language they have learned from the Student Book and video narration.

The worksheet on page 87 of this Teacher's Guide may be photocopied and given to students to complete either while they view the video, or after they have finished the **Explore More** viewing task.

Exploring Further: Reading and Viewing

How else can students improve their reading skills and increase their awareness of the world?

1. The review units in *Reading Explorer* further develop learners' reading skills and visual literacy through the use of graphic images such as charts, diagrams, maps, and symbols. In addition, one of the aims of *Reading Explorer* includes motivating students to learn about the world and its cultures. Features of the course that promote these goals are:

- Review units which contain **Spotlights** on UNESCO (United Nations Educational, Scientific, and Cultural Organization) World Heritage Sites and **Global View** pages which highlight important global issues, such as water and world trade
- Extensive reading on related topics through the *Footprint Reading Library*
- *Reading Explorer* website with student search activities and downloadable materials for teachers

The review units highlight well-known places of outstanding cultural or natural importance that have been designated UNESCO World Heritage Sites. Features of the review units include:

- Full-color, two-page spreads with maps and 3-D drawings
- Descriptions of unique features
- Information on location and status
- Glossary of special terms (highlighted in blue in the text)
- Field Notes sections that summarize facts about the sites

The worksheets on pages 88–89 of this Teacher's Guide may be photocopied and given to students before or after they read each World Heritage Spotlight and Global View section.

2. The *Footprint Reading Library* is a series of graded readers produced through collaboration between Heinle Cengage Learning and National Geographic. *Footprint* readers, audio, and visual materials are controlled for vocabulary and grammatical structures appropriate for learners' proficiency levels. See page 96 of this Teacher's Guide for suggested extensive readers from the *Footprint Reading Library* for each unit.

3. Both teachers and learners are encouraged to use the *Reading Explorer* website (elt.heinle.com) for further independent reading and exploration opportunities, and also National Geographic's main website: Nationalgeographic.com. The National Geographic website offers many short videos on topics closely related to *Reading Explorer* topics. These videos provide opportunities for independent learning and extension activities.

Assessing Learners' Progress

How can learners' progress be assessed with *Reading Explorer*?

Ongoing assessment with *Reading Explorer* allows teachers to obtain feedback on students' progress in vocabulary, reading skills, and visual literacy. Ways that teachers can assess learners include:

- Reading comprehension questions that reflect current question formats on standardized English exams
- Vocabulary practice and review sections that check learners' understanding of recently acquired vocabulary
- Photocopiable worksheets for students to complete as they complete the reading and viewing tasks (see pages 86–89 of this Teacher's Guide)
- Self-grading vocabulary activities and reading and viewing comprehension questions on the Student CD-ROM
- Web search activities that enable teachers to monitor students' progress in learning independently
- Assessment CD-ROM with Exam*View*® so teachers can quickly create customized tests

The Exam*View*® software provided with *Reading Explorer* contains banks of questions on readings and vocabulary for each unit. The questions mirror many of the types and formats of questions used in the Student Book. With Exam*View*®, teachers can create and customize exams quickly and easily.

The Exam*View*® component provides the following question banks for each unit of *Reading Explorer*:

- An additional reading passage related to the unit topic with 10 comprehension questions
- A bank of 10 questions relating to the target vocabulary of Lesson A
- A bank of 10 questions relating to the target vocabulary of Lesson B

The questions cover a variety of task types, including multiple-choice, true/false, and completion. The reading comprehension questions focus on the same range of reading skills that are highlighted in the Student Book, for example, understanding main ideas, details, and inferences, identifying references, and understanding vocabulary from context.

Unit Introduction

This unit focuses on food in different cultures. Students will read about olive oil cultivation and production in the Mediterranean and then discover *sofrito*, a popular sauce in Puerto Rico.

Key Words for Internet Research: *Caribbean, ethnic foods, food and culture, foreign cuisine, Mediterranean, Naxos, olive oil, Puerto Rico, Taíno cuisine, Thai cuisine, trans fats, world foods*

For More Information: http://www.nationalgeographicfood.com/

Warm Up

Answer Key

Answers will vary.

Teaching Notes

Write the words *chef* and *wok* on the board and pronounce them [sheff, walk]. Note that the second *e* in the word *vegetables* is almost silent. Tell students to look at the photo and read the caption. Ask them:

- **What are the people in the photo doing?** They are student cooks or *chefs*, learning how to cook vegetables.
- **What is a *wok*?** It is a deep, round-bottom metal pan used primarily in cooking Asian foods.
- **What do you call this kind of cooking?** Stir-frying—in which the chef constantly stirs or moves the food being cooked.
- **Where is Hefei?** Hefei is the capital of Anhui Province situated in eastern China. The region was known for agriculture in the past, so good cooking was important there.
- **Why are the students wearing special clothes?** Chefs wear a special uniform that identifies them and protects them from spills and stains. They are wearing a high hat known as a *toque* [tock] on their head for sanitary purposes.

Lesson 1A — The Home of the Olive

Lesson Overview

Target Vocabulary:

account (for), approximately, associated (with), attackers, ceremony, civilization, evidence, initially, liquid, process

Reading Passage Summary:

Read about the history, production, benefits, and use of olive oil.

Answer Key

Before You Read

A. 1. separate; **2.** enhance; **3.** cultivate; **4.** harvest; **5.** produce

B. b. the history and benefits of olive oil

Reading Comprehension

A. 1. d; **2.** c (lines 5–6); **3.** b (line 11); **4.** d (lines 26 and 29); **5.** a (paragraph 5)

B. Inside the Mediterranean Region: a and d; Outside the Mediterranean Region: b; Both: c and e

Vocabulary Practice

A. 1. accounts for; **2.** associated with; **3.** approximately; **4.** evidence; **5.** process

B. 1. d; **2.** a; **3.** e; **4.** c; **5.** b

Teaching Notes

Before You Read

A. Completion: Direct students' attention to the map key and ask what the two colors mean (present-day extent of olive production and places where cultivation started long ago). Ask about the context of the map by having students point to Europe, North Africa, the Middle East, the Atlantic Ocean, and the Black Sea. Remind students that the sentences may require a different form of the words in blue. Have them complete Activity A and then ask which words changed their form. Which ones changed the part of speech? (*cultivation* and *producers* became verbs instead of nouns)

B. Skim for the Main Idea: Have students quickly read the title, photo captions, and paragraph 1 to determine the main idea. Then have them skim the entire passage, including the captions and labels. Point out that the olive at the bottom of page 11 is actually a chart that shows the percentage of olive oil production among the world's leading olive oil producers.

Reading Comprehension

A. Multiple Choice: Have students read the entire passage silently and answer the questions for Activity A. Check answers as a class and have students give evidence for their answers using line references from the reading. Question 2 requires students to interpret time and sequence using information from paragraph 1. Remind students that 2,000 years ago was a dividing line between B.C. and A.D., so 4000 B.C. is really 6,000 years ago. Draw a timeline on the board with the most important dates.

B. Classification: Have students complete Activity B. Check answers as a class.

Challenge: For students who have completed Activities A and B, write the following questions on the board. Additional comprehension questions are available on the CD-ROM.
1. Are olives eaten in your culture? Do you like them?
2. Do you think olive oil is the secret to good health? Are there other things about the Mediterranean diet and lifestyle that might be healthy? For example, eating a lot of fish, but few sweets.

Vocabulary Practice

A. Completion: Have students do Activity A. Then, have students check answers with a partner.

B. Definitions: Have students do Activity B. Check answers as a class. Then ask them to form an example sentence for each of the five words.

Challenge: Ask students who have completed Activities A and B to talk quietly about the illustration of the food label on page 14. Are foods labeled this way in their country? How can reading labels help you to choose healthy foods?

Word Partnership

Evidence is information that proves something is true or has really happened. People who use evidence in their daily work include scientists, the police, and lawyers. Make three columns on the board headed by these three occupations. Ask students what kind of evidence each person uses. For example, information that ice caps are melting would be useful for a scientist studying global warming. A gun with fingerprints from a crime site would be useful to both a policeman and a lawyer in solving a murder.

A Taste of the Caribbean

Lesson Overview

Target Vocabulary:

aspect, assumption, base, contrasting, immigration, import, invade, layered, occasionally, remarkable

Reading Passage Summary:

Historically, there have been many different cultural influences on Puerto Rican food, one of which is *sofrito*, a popular base for many Puerto Rican dishes.

Answer Key

Before You Read

A. From top to bottom: 4, 5, 1, 3, 2
B. 1. It is a sauce or base for other dishes; 2. Onion, garlic, green bell peppers, sweet chili peppers, cilantro, olive oil, and oregano

Reading Comprehension

A. 1. a (lines 5–6); 2. b (paragraph 2); 3. b (line 4); 4. c (line 24); 5. b (line 28)
B. 1. T; 2. F; 3. F; 4. F; 5. T; 6. T; 7. F

Vocabulary Practice

A. 1. aspect; 2. occasionally; 3. imported; 4. base; 5. layers
B. 1. invaded; 2. contrasting; 3. assumption; 4. immigration; 5. Remarkably

Teaching Notes

Before You Read

A. Matching: Have students circle words in the descriptions that help identify the foods in the pictures. Some examples are *chips*, *shellfish*, *rice*, and *dessert*. *Yams* may be found through the process of elimination after the clues are used for the other pictures.

B. Scan: Have students *scan* for specific information. Some common kinds of dishes are meats, pasta, snacks, and desserts. A *base* is the foundation for other things, so *sofrito* is a sauce that gives flavor to dishes using vegetables, meat, or fish. Ingredients are given in lines 26–27 and 30–36.

Reading Comprehension

A. Multiple Choice: Have students read the entire passage silently and answer the questions for Activity A. Check answers as a class. Note that this passage has two sections—a description of Puerto Rico's history and cuisine followed by a recipe. Question 1 deals with the sequence of cultures in Puerto Rico. Draw a timeline on the board with the following points: before 1500, 1508, soon after 1508, 1898. Point out that in 1898 Puerto Rico became attached to the United States. Ask where

to put the following cultures: Taíno, Spanish, and African. For Question 4, have students pay attention to the sentence in line 24. The word *however* signals a change from the previous sentence that describes hot or spicy chili peppers. Even if students don't know the word *milder*, they can deduce that the example of *sofrito* is different.

B. True or False: Have students decide whether the statements are true or false. Most statements are straightforward, but item 4 requires inference. The instructions say "Place a heavy-bottomed pot over low heat," which implies cooking on a stove, and not in an oven.

Challenge: Have students work in groups of four. They pretend to have a TV cooking show in which they demonstrate, step by step, how to make *sofrito*.

Vocabulary Practice

A. Definitions: Have students do Activity A. Point out that *occasionally* appears on a continuum of adverbs of frequency. Draw a line on the board and fill in some of these adverbs and let the class supply others: *always*, *never*, *sometimes*, *rarely*, *usually*, *seldom*, *often*, and *occasionally.* Then, have students check answers with a partner.

B. Completion: As students complete the paragraph, ask them to pay attention to the part of speech needed for each gap. This will help them to use the correct form of words. Other cues to be aware of include the *a(n)* choice for articles before nouns and the gap that occurs at the start of a sentence.

Challenge: For students who have completed Activities A and B, write the following questions on the board. Additional vocabulary questions are available on the CD-ROM.
1. Which Thai sweet would you like to try? Why?
2. In your opinion, did Taíno civilization die out? Explain your answer.

Usage

English has several words that are pronounced differently according to their use as a noun or verb. Like *contrast*, the words *record* and *produce* are pronounced with the accent on the first syllable when used as a noun. As a verb, the accent is on the second syllable.

Explore More

Video Summary: The humble olive tree has been an important part of life in Greece for thousands of years, providing food, shelter, and even peace in the form of an olive branch.

Answer Key

A. 1. F; **2.** T; **3.** F
B. 1. initially; **2.** assumption; **3.** processed;
    4. accounts for; **5.** civilization; **6.** associated;
    7. aspect; **8.** remarkable; **9.** evidence; **10.** liquid
C. 1. It is useful for cooking and enhancing health.
    2. Possible answers: green tea and red wine

Teaching Notes

A. Preview: For suggestions on building students' viewing skills, see pages 19–20. Have students look at the photo and read the caption. Ask students to complete Activity A. Have students brainstorm any words or ideas they associate with olives. Write their ideas on the board and return to check them after viewing the video.

Some ideas may be:
- Different colored olives come from the same tree. The color indicates how ripe they are.
- Olives have been important in Mediterranean civilization for thousands of years.
- Individual olive trees can live for a very long time.
- Olives and olive oil are believed to have health benefits.
- The olive tree is associated with peace.

B. Summarize: Follow these steps:
1. Students watch the video through once, bearing in mind the answers they gave in the **Preview**.
2. Before playing the video a second time, ask students to read the summary and fill the gaps in Activity B with vocabulary items from the box. They close their books while watching the video.
3. After they've watched the video a second time, students complete or change their answers on the summary. Have them check answers with a partner.
4. If necessary, play the video through a third time and then check answers as a class.

C. Think About It: Have students answer the questions in Activity C in pairs. Discuss ideas as a class.

Unit 2 | Animals and Language

Unit Introduction

This unit focuses on animal communication with examples of humpback whale songs and the interaction between dogs and humans.

Key Words for Internet Research: *animal communication, animal language, dog training, humpback whale song, singing whales, whale migration, working dogs*

For More Information: http://animals.nationalgeographic.com/animals

Warm Up

Answer Key

1. Scientists who have studied animal intelligence say that primates such as chimpanzees and gorillas top the list, followed by dolphins, elephants, and pigs. **2.** Animals communicate with sounds, body positions, and movements. **3.** Answers will vary.

Teaching Notes

Write the word *zebra* on the board and pronounce it [zee bra]. Tell students to look at the photo and read the caption. Ask them:

- **What do you know about zebras?** They are related to horses and donkeys but live only in Africa. Each zebra has a different stripe pattern.
- **What are the zebras in the photo doing?** They are making noises to communicate. Zebras make barking noises in addition to whinnying like a horse or braying like a donkey.
- **What is Masai Mara, and where is it?** It is a game reserve in Kenya, named for the Masai people who live there near the Mara River.

Lesson 2A | Ocean Giants

Lesson Overview

Target Vocabulary:

alarmed, awareness, complex, constantly, curiously, enemy, harm, interact, unknown, variety

Reading Passage Summary:

Read about humpback whales and explore research findings about their songs and singing habits.

Answer Key

Before You Read

A. a. 2; **b.** 1; **c.** 3
B. Humpback whales are intelligent, lighthearted, and active at the surface of the water, and swim close to land.

Reading Comprehension

A. 1. b; **2.** d (line 23); **3.** d; **4.** b (line 25); **5.** a (line 36)
B. 1. b; **2.** c; **3.** e; **4.** d; **5.** a

Vocabulary Practice

A. 1. interacting; **2.** complex; **3.** enemies; **4.** variety; **5.** curious
B. 1. constantly; **2.** alarmed; **3.** harmed; **4.** awareness; **5.** unknown

Teaching Notes

Before You Read

A. Matching: Before they read the descriptions, have students look carefully at the photos and say what they see. Do they see one, two, or many whales? What do they think the whales are doing? Ask what *flippers* and *schools* mean in this context. Do students know other meanings for these words? If so, how are they similar or different to these uses? Have students do Activity A and check answers as a class.

B. Predict: Have students guess why humpback whales are popular with whale watchers. Ask if anyone has watched whales. Then have students read paragraph 1, pointing out the explanation for *lighthearted* at the bottom of page 23.

Reading Comprehension

A. Multiple Choice: Draw students' attention to the map and caption on page 24. Write the word *migration* on the board and explain that it means movement from one place to another. In this case, humpbacks spend the summer months in cold waters in the north of Russia, Alaska, and Canada. In the winter, they migrate to warmer waters where they breed or mate and the female whales give birth. There are three different migration patterns. Have students describe where each group of whales travels. Is there anywhere all three groups meet? (Alaska) Then, have students read the entire passage silently and answer the questions for Activity A. Check answers as a class, asking students to give evidence for their answers using line references from the passage.

B. Matching: Have students complete Activity B, and then check answers as a class. Ask students how definite or certain each number is, pointing out the modifiers *estimated*, *around*, *perhaps*, and *more*.

Only the statement about how long Jim Darling has studied humpbacks is definite.

Challenge: For students who have completed Activities A and B, write the following question on the board. Additional comprehension questions are available on the CD-ROM.

On page 23 is a picture of a photographer close to a mother whale. Do you think it is dangerous to get that close to a humpback whale? Give reasons for your answer.

Vocabulary Practice

A. Definitions: Have students do Activity A. Then, have students check answers with a partner.

B. Completion: Have students do Activity B. Check answers as a class.

Challenge: Have students who have completed Activities A and B use captions from photos throughout the unit and make up questions to ask other students. For example: What is the largest whale? (blue whale, photo on page 26) Note that at http://animals.nationalgeographic.com/animals/, students can select humpback or blue whales from the pull-down alphabetical list on the right and listen to their songs.

Usage

Ask for examples of both words used as nouns, verbs, and adjectives. Note the collocation of other words with them. Some examples are: *sound the alarm*, *an alarming trend*, *set my alarm* (short for alarm clock) *for six*, *do bodily harm*, *harmful to your health*, and *in harm's way*.

Our Bond with Dogs

Lesson Overview

Target Vocabulary:

acquired, domestic, garbage, government, luggage, obedient, partnership, plenty, selection, talents

Reading Passage Summary:

Read about three types of dogs that play very different roles in human society.

Answer Key

Before You Read

A. Answers will vary.
B. 1. Jacques, a beagle; **2.** Tiffy, a Maltese; **3.** Jessie, a whippet

Reading Comprehension

A. 1. c; **2.** b (paragraph 1); **3.** b (line 9); **4.** c (lines 40); **5.** a (lines 33–35)
B. 1. Tiffy: d and e; **2.** Jacques: c; **3.** Jessie: b; **4.** Both Jessie and Jacques: a

Vocabulary Practice

A. 1. luggage; **2.** garbage; **3.** government; **4.** domestic; **5.** partnership
B. 1. acquire; **2.** obedient; **3.** talent; **4.** plenty; **5.** selection

Teaching Notes

Before You Read

A. Discussion: 1. From left to right, the types of dogs are: bullmastiff, Pomeranian, Old English sheepdog, Miniature poodle, Great Dane, Chihuahua, bulldog, greyhound, Doberman pinscher, longhaired dachshund, and Siberian husky. **2.** The sheepdog is a herder, the greyhound is used for racing, the Doberman is used as a guard dog, and the Siberian husky pulls sleds. **3.** The bullmastiff and Doberman pinscher are fierce, the Great Dane is very gentle, the greyhound runs very fast, and the Siberian husky can cope with Arctic weather. **4.** Answers will vary. **5.** Answers will vary.

B. Scan: Each dog is named and its breed is described under the three headings.

Reading Comprehension

A. Multiple Choice: Have students read the entire passage silently and answer the questions for Activity A. Check answers as a class, asking students to give evidence for their answers using line references from the passage. Draw students' attention to the headings for each section. Ask what they mean and why each dog is well suited to its task. The photos and captions provide helpful information. For Question 2, note that three of the options can be found in paragraph 1. Although students can answer the question by the process of elimination, encourage them to read the entire passage before answering.

B. Classification: While students have encountered two-ring Venn diagrams before, here the Venn diagrams have three rings, one for each dog. There are more possibilities for overlap, between each two dogs and then an area in the middle that would apply to all three dogs. Ask students to think of other things from the passage that could go into the overlapping areas. Which dogs work outside the home? Which are small dogs? Which dogs are affectionate?

Challenge: For students who have completed Activities A and B, write the following question on the board. Additional comprehension questions are available on the CD-ROM.

Of all the dogs in the unit, which make the best pets for a family? Explain your answer.

Vocabulary Practice

A. Matching: Have students do Activity A. Then, have students check answers with a partner.

B. Completion: As students complete the paragraph, ask them to pay attention to the part of speech needed for each gap. This will help them to use the correct form of words.

Challenge: For students who have completed Activities A and B, write the following questions on the board. Additional vocabulary questions are available on the CD-ROM.
1. What working dogs have you known? What did they do?
2. Do you think a guard dog can ever be trusted to be gentle?

Explore More

Video Summary: Learn about the special relationship between dog and man, and how these loyal animals came to be Man's Best Friend.

Answer Key

A. a. 2; **b.** 1; **c.** 4; **d.** 3
B. 1. partnership; **2.** variety; **3.** plenty; **4.** talent;
  5. luggage; **6.** obedient; **7.** interacting; **8.** unknown;
  9. selection; **10.** domestic

C. 1. Dogs are used for search-and-rescue to locate people after disasters, they herd and manage livestock such as sheep, they serve as guides for people with handicaps such as blindness, and they find and retrieve game for hunters.
2. Many other domestic animals such as cats and horses have a close bond with people.

Teaching Notes

A. Preview: For suggestions on building students' viewing skills, see pages 19–20. Have students look at the photos and read the captions. Ask students to complete Activity A. Brainstorm about what students know about the animals pictured. Write their ideas on the board and return to check them after viewing the video. Some ideas may be:
- Wolves are wild relatives of dogs. They were hated and hunted for many years, but now wolves are protected in some places.
- Huskies are sled dogs. They work in a team to pull sleds over long distances in the Arctic.
- Border collies have a natural talent for herding or organizing other animals. At dog shows, they even have herding competitions to see which border collies are most efficient.
- Beagles, like Jacques in the passage, have a keen sense of smell and so are often used by police and security as "sniffer dogs" at airports.

B. Summarize: Follow these steps:
1. Students watch the video through once, bearing in mind the answers they gave in the **Preview**.
2. Before playing the video a second time, ask students to read the summary and fill the gaps in Activity B with vocabulary items from the box. They close their books while watching the video.
3. After they've watched the video a second time, students complete or change their answers on the summary. Have them check answers with a partner.
4. If necessary, play the video through a third time and then check answers as a class.

C. Think About It: Have students answer the questions in Activity C in pairs. Discuss ideas as a class.

Unit Introduction

This unit explores two historical murder mysteries: the death of Egyptian King Tut and what happened to the Iceman in the Italian Alps over 5,300 years ago.

Key Words for Internet Research: *ancient Egypt, Inca civilization, Inca mummy, King Tutankhamun, mummies, pharaohs, the Iceman, Valley of the Kings*

For More Information: http://ngm.nationalgeographic.com/ngm/0506/feature1/ and http://ngm.nationalgeographic.com/2007/07/iceman/hall-text

Warm Up

Answer Key

1. Answers will vary. **2.** Researchers learn about the past from written records and physical remains such as the ruins of buildings, equipment or personal possessions that have survived, and sometimes human bodies. **3.** Possible answers: Egyptian, Mesopotamian, Greek, Roman, Aztec, and Incan. They are famous for their art and architecture, including their tombs.

Teaching Notes

Write the word *mummy* on the board and ask what students know about ancient mummies. A *mummy* is a dead body that has been preserved using chemicals or by accidental exposure to extreme cold and low humidity. Tell students to look at the photo on page 33 and read the caption. Ask them:
- **What are the people in the photo doing?** They are putting the mummy of King Tutankhamun through a medical CT scanner.
- **What is a *CT scanner*?** It is a machine that makes it possible to look inside the human body to see bones and organs.
- **Why scan the mummy of King Tutankhamun?** Archeologists wanted to learn more about his health and how he died.

Lesson 3A | Secrets of the Pharaohs

Lesson Overview

Target Vocabulary:

analyze, attach, conduct, exclude, infection, injury, luxurious, murder, teenager, theory

Reading Passage Summary:

Discover how modern technology is used to solve the mystery of King Tutankhamun's death in 1322 B.C.

Answer Key

Before You Read

A. From top to bottom: tomb; coffin; mummy; Archeologist
B. Theories include murder, an injury from war or a hunting accident, or an infection from a knee fracture.

Reading Comprehension

A. 1. c (line 52); **2.** b; **3.** c (lines 25–27); **4.** a (line 32); **5.** d (line 51)
B. From left to right: 5, 2, 3, 1, 4

Vocabulary Practice

A. 1. luxurious; **2.** theory; **3.** exclude; **4.** conducted; **5.** injuries
B. 1. infected; **2.** analysis; **3.** murder; **4.** teenagers; **5.** attachment

Teaching Notes

Before You Read

A. Completion: Direct students' attention to the globe and map. Tell students that the star symbol next to Cairo means it is the capital city of Egypt. Note the location of the Valley of the Kings near Luxor. Ask what direction you would travel to it from Cairo. Ask students to examine the photos carefully. A *coffin* is the box in which a dead body is buried or cremated while a *tomb* is a larger structure or building that contains the coffin. See the photo on page 35 for the complex way King Tutankhamun was buried.

B. Scan: Remind students that they are to read the passage as quickly as possible, looking for information about how King Tut died. After one minute, have students close their books and tell what they learned. If there is any uncertain information, have students check back in the passage.

Reading Comprehension

A. Multiple Choice: Have students read the entire passage silently and answer the questions for Activity A. Check answers as a class, asking students to give evidence for their answers using line references from the reading passage.

B. Matching: Students have to place events on a timeline running from the oldest events on the left side to the most recent events on the right. Note the break in the timeline, which indicates that it is not to scale. Have students complete Activity B. Check answers as a class.

Challenge: After finishing Activities A and B, have all students focus on the other photos, illustrations, and ***Did You Know?*** in the unit before answering the following questions. Additional comprehension questions are available on the CD-ROM.

1. Why do you think archeologist Zahi Hawass was shocked when he saw King Tut's face?
2. What animal does the Anubis costume look like?
3. Where is the mummy of King Tutankhamun now?

Vocabulary Practice

A. Completion: Have students do Activity A. Then, have students check answers with a partner. Note that *conduct* is often used together with business. When scientists *conduct an experiment*, they organize the research and carry it out. You can also conduct tests or conduct research.

B. Completion: Have students do Activity B. Check answers as a class.

Challenge: Ask students to write a paragraph about what they think the love poem on page 38 means.

Word Link

Teenager technically refers to anyone aged between 13 and 19. Start a class discussion about whether there really is one special "teenage market" with its own music, magazines, movies, clothing, and so on, and whether there is a big difference between young teens and those who are 18 or 19. For example, many older teens have completed high school and are now in university or are employed.

Lesson 3B — A Body in the Mountains

Lesson Overview

Target Vocabulary:

beneath, cruelly, debatable, deduce, enable, frozen, imply, laborer, tiny, wealth

Reading Passage Summary:

Investigation of the Iceman, a frozen mummy found in the Italian Alps, gives clues about his life and death 5,300 years ago.

Answer Key

Before You Read

A. 1. c; **2.** b; **3.** c
B. Answers will vary.

Reading Comprehension

A. 1. b; **2.** d (lines 14–15); **3.** c (lines 37–40);
    4. b (line 43); **5.** a (line 49)
B. 1. F; **2.** T; **3.** T; **4.** F; **5.** F

Vocabulary Practice

A. 1. cruelly; **2.** wealth; **3.** laborer; **4.** tiny; **5.** debatable
B. 1. beneath; **2.** deduce; **3.** frozen; **4.** implies;
    5. enables

Teaching Notes

Before You Read

A. Discussion: Have students work in pairs to use the information from the Police Report, the photos, and the captions to answer the questions. Questions 2 and 3 require inference. For Question 2, the deep cuts on the Iceman suggest that his death was not natural. For Question 3, students should take note of the tools and weapons the Iceman was carrying. The questions help students predict what they will read later.

B. Scan: Have students read quickly for specific information to check their answers to Activity A. They can get the answer to Question 1 from the Police Report, but they should focus on how the Iceman died and the dark shape under his shoulder to check answers to Questions 2 and 3.

Reading Comprehension

A. Multiple Choice: Have students read the entire passage silently and answer the questions for Activity A. Check answers as a class, asking students to give evidence for their answers using line references from the reading passage. Encourage students to explore the passage more carefully, especially to understand the vocabulary items *imply* (suggest in an indirect way that something is true) and *deduce* (reach a conclusion based on other things that are true). Use the following questions to illustrate the two processes mentioned:

- **How did the Iceman's body remain in perfect condition?** The extreme cold and ice preserved his body.
- **What implies that the Iceman wasn't a laborer?** His arms don't have a laborer's muscles.
- **What implies that the Iceman was wealthy?** He had a copper axe, something rare and valuable in those times.
- **How can scientists deduce where he lived in Italy?** They could analyze the foods in his stomach. They know that some foods don't grow high in the mountains.
- **Why do scientists deduce that he was murdered?** The stone arrow is evidence.

B. Fact or Theory: Note that most students have experience with true/false questions where T stands for true and F for false. Here, the letters are exactly reversed. T is for a theory, something that may be a good explanation but has not been proven. F is for a proven fact. Discuss the concepts of *theory* and *fact* before students do Activity B. Check answers as a class.

Challenge: Have students work in pairs. Have each person tell their partner one fact, one theory, and one false statement about the Iceman. Can the partner tell which is which?

Vocabulary Practice

A. Completion: Have students do Activity A. Then, have students check answers with a partner.

B. Definitions: Have students do Activity B. Then, check answers as a class and ask, for example, sentences using the vocabulary words.

Challenge: For students who have completed Activities A and B, write the following question on the board. Additional vocabulary questions are available on the CD-ROM.

If you had been hiking in the Alps and found the Iceman, what would you have done?

Word Partnership

If something can be *debated*, it can be discussed because it is a subject on which people have different views. If something is *open to debate*, it is also *open to discussion* or suggestions from other points of view.

Explore More

Video Summary: An important discovery is made when a mummified young Inca girl turns out to be one of many human sacrifices.

Answer Key

A. b. She was sacrificed to the mountain god.
B. 1. conducting; **2.** deduce; **3.** murdered; **4.** theory; **5.** analyzed; **6.** injury; **7.** beneath; **8.** enable; **9.** frozen; **10.** attached

C. 1. Possible answer: They can learn what people looked like, what they wore, their health and diet, and perhaps some things about their belief system. **2.** For further information about the Inca or other past civilizations, see the Mysteries of the Ancient World section at http://www.nationalgeographic. com/history/ and use the pull-down menu on the top right of the webpage.

Teaching Notes

A. Preview: For suggestions on building students' viewing skills, see pages 19–20. Have students look at the photo and read the caption. Ask students to complete Activity A. Elicit what students know about Inca civilization. Write their ideas on the board and return to check them after viewing the video. Some ideas may be:

- The Inca Empire was in the Andes Mountains in South America in today's Ecuador, Peru, Bolivia, and Chile.
- Its high point was between 1200 A.D. and 1500 A.D. when the Spanish arrived.
- The Inca were famous for their stone cities like Machu Picchu.
- The Inca used knotted strings called *quipu* to record information, instead of writing.
- Spanish invaders sought gold and silver from the Inca. Although the civilization fell, some of the culture survives in the people of the Andes.

B. Summarize: Follow these steps:
1. Students watch the video through once, bearing in mind the answers they gave in the **Preview**.
2. Before playing the video a second time, ask students to read the summary and fill the gaps in Activity B with vocabulary items from the box. Have them close their books while watching the video.
3. After they've watched the video a second time, students complete or change their answers on the summary. Have them check answers with a partner.
4. If necessary, play the video through a third time and then check answers as a class.

C. Think About It: Have students answer the questions in Activity C in pairs. Discuss ideas as a class.

Answer Key

A. Across: 1. complex; **3.** infect; **5.** variety; **7.** imply; **8.** civilization; **11.** remarkable; **13.** tiny; **14.** domestic;
15. harm; **16.** wealth; **17.** analyze; **18.** import
Down: **1.** contrast; **2.** exclude; **4.** talent; **6.** evidence; **8.** ceremony; **9.** interact; **10.** beneath; **12.** assume

B. Pompeii, Italy, 25,000, Vesuvius, August 24, ash, indoor pools, theater, palaestra/sports, mid-18th

Teaching Notes

A. Crossword: Before students attempt the crossword in Activity A, have them review the vocabulary from Units 1 through 3 using the **Target Vocabulary** list on pages 177–178 where words are given with unit numbers. Then, have students use the definitions to complete the crossword. They should fill in the words they know first, using letters as clues for more challenging items. Check answers as a class.

B. Notes Completion: Have students do Activity B. Check answers as a class.

World Heritage Spotlight: Pompeii and Herculaneum

Background Information

The Roman cities of Pompeii and Herculaneum were destroyed by an eruption of Mount Vesuvius in 79 A.D. They are located southeast of Naples, Italy. Ash and pumice stone from the volcano covered the cities so quickly that people did not have time to flee to safety. They were caught in their everyday activities. For this reason, when the site was finally excavated by archeologists 1,700 years later, details of life were extremely well preserved. *Frescoes* or wall paintings tell researchers about daily life and the religious beliefs of that time.

Geologists who have analyzed the soil believe that Vesuvius erupted in 1780 B.C. In addition, there are signs that a terrible earthquake occurred in 62 A.D., only 17 years before the destruction of the cities. People must have been optimistic that a further disaster would not occur, because they had worked hard to rebuild damaged buildings. Yet, when the eruption happened in 79 A.D., the victims were caught and they died immediately. The historian Pliny the Younger—quoted on page 46—saw the disaster and lost his uncle who died trying to save people.

Today, Pompeii is a UNESCO World Heritage Site, and scientists and historians are concerned that some of the site is being destroyed by its exposure to the air and by too much tourism. They have closed off some of Pompeii for further excavation and have tried to get tourists to visit other sites in the area such as Herculaneum instead of only Pompeii.

For More Information: http://www.nationalgeographic. com/history/ancient/pompeii.html, http://ngm. nationalgeographic.com/2007/09/vesuvius/eruption-interactive, and http://whc.unesco.org/en/list/829/video

Teaching Notes

Overview: The spread on pages 46–47 has many features. A photo of what Pompeii looks like today is in the center of the spread with Mount Vesuvius in the background. The buildings in the foreground are those of the ancient city. On the right is an artist's reconstruction of what Herculaneum might have looked like just before Mount Vesuvius erupted.

- The numbers in blue circles are keyed to the features described in the box about Herculaneum.
- The yellow box on the upper left side of page 46 gives information about the World Heritage Site. The globe indicates the ancient cities' location in Italy near the Mediterranean Sea.

- The white box on page 46 gives an overview of what happened in Pompeii in 79 A.D.
- The gray box on page 46 tells about an earlier disaster in 1780 B.C.
- A glossary for unfamiliar terms is in the yellow box on page 47.
- The blue box next to the photo on page 47 tells about ongoing work in uncovering and analyzing the ancient remains. The archeologist is using a toothbrush to remove dirt and ash.

Teaching Suggestions: Allow each student time to explore the features on pages 46–47. Then, brainstorm what students see on those pages and make a list on the board. Explain that there are many important dates in the text and that the class is going to make a *timeline*.

Making a Timeline

Draw a long horizontal line on the board and label it with those dates, but do not write what happened on those dates. From left to right, the dates are
- **25,000 years ago:** Mount Vesuvius is formed
- **1780 B.C.:** Mount Vesuvius erupts
- **79 A.D.:** Mount Vesuvius erupts again, destroying Pompeii and Herculaneum
- **112:** Pliny the Younger dies

- **1750:** mid-18th century, Pompeii rediscovered
- **1997:** the ancient cities become World Heritage Sites
- **Today:** analysis of the ancient cities continues

Ask students to find information on pages 46–47 for each date and write it above the date.

Reading Illustrations

An important part of visual literacy is "reading" photographs and illustrations. In this case, the illustration of Herculaneum is marked with numbers to locate important buildings. Write the Latin words *basilica* [bah **sill** ik ah] and *palaestra* [pal **ess** trah] on the board and pronounce them. Then, ask questions like these:
- **Where would you go to get help on legal issues?** The basilica, number 2
- **Where could you have a hot bath?** Number 6
- **If you wanted to see a race, where would you go?** The palaestra, number 3
- **What buildings are at the edge of the city?** Numbers 1 and 2

Challenge: Scientists say Mount Vesuvius erupts about every 2,000 years. Do you think it's safe for people to live near the volcano today? Explain your reasons.

A Global View: Languages

Background Knowledge

To prepare students for the language topic, ask some of the following questions:
- What languages do people in the class speak?
- What families do these languages belong to?
- If students speak several languages, which language did they learn first?

- Can students speak and understand any languages without reading or writing them?
- Why learn English as a second language?

Teaching Notes

Overview: The Indo-European language family includes most European languages—Russian; Iranian or Persian; and a number of Indian languages such as Sanskrit, Hindi, Bengali, and Urdu. As speakers of Indo-European languages migrated to or colonized other areas, these languages spread. For example, English is now a first language throughout much of North America and Australia, and Spanish is a first language from Mexico to the tip of South America. The Sino-Tibetan language family includes Mandarin as well as languages spoken in Tibet, Burma, and Southeast Asia.

Key Words for Internet Research: *dead languages*, *endangered languages*, *English as an international language*, *language families*, *native speaker*

For More Information: http://en.wikipedia.org/wiki/List_of_language_families and http://www.livingtongues.org/

Building Graphic Literacy

Map Reading

The map on pages 48–49 shows the extent of major language families today. Draw attention to the map key and ask students where major language families are found. Can they name some of the languages? As students work through the list, point out the colored information boxes. The box about Native American languages is in the "Other" category. Ask about other places coded with this color. They include the Caucasus region between the Black and Caspian seas, Southwest Africa, Central Australia, and the Kamchatka Peninsula of Russia.

Have students work in groups of four to write questions about the map or the information boxes. Put the questions in a bag or box, mix them up, and have groups take turns selecting questions to answer.

Bar Charts

The bar chart at the bottom of page 48 shows the number of native speakers in millions of various languages. Spanish, English, Hindi, Portuguese (also spoken in Brazil), Bengali (spoken in India and Bangladesh), Russian, and German are all included in the Indo-European language family. The bars measure *native speakers*—people who learned these languages as mother tongues. Ask students the following questions to check comprehension of the bar chart:

- **Which has more native speakers, Spanish or English? Why?** Spanish countries have large populations. Both languages spread from Europe during a time of colonization.
- **Which language on the chart has the fewest speakers?** German
- **Which languages on the graph use the same basic writing system?** Spanish, English, Portuguese, and German

Line Graphs

The line graph at the bottom of page 49 shows the number of languages in thousands and the world's population over a period of time. To use a line graph, students need to find the point where the variables *intersect*. Use a ruler or other straight edge to find points on the line.

The purple line shows changes in the world's population over time. It indicates slow growth to 1500, moderate growth to 1990 and a huge amount of growth after that. The final date is 91 years in the future, so that information is projected, not actual. The top of the green-shaded area indicates a pattern with the number of languages. It shows a decline from about 12,000 languages at 10,000 B.C. to about 4,000 today. Ask students the following questions to check understanding of the line graph:

- **How many languages were there in 1500 A.D.?** About 9,000
- **How many people were there in 1500 A.D.?** Less than 1 billion
- **What is the world's population today?** About 6 billion

Vocabulary in Context

Finding *appositions* is a strategy to figure out the meaning of words from their contexts. Appositions (students don't need to know the term, only the concept) are two consecutive noun phrases where the second provides a definition or synonym for the first. In the yellow box find *linguists*, people who study and analyze languages. Under Top Ten Languages, find *native speakers* (people who learned it as a first language rather than as a foreign language). Ask learners to find the meanings of *dead languages* and *characters*. Note that appositions are set off in different ways: commas, parentheses, dashes, and with the conjunction *or*.

Word Partnership

The word *language* pairs with many words, sometimes as a noun and sometimes as an adjective. Ask for examples other than those given on page 49. Some possibilities are: *native language*, *first language*, *second language*, *language course*, *language skills*, *speak a language*.

Critical Thinking

A language dies when there are no more people who can understand or speak it. It is a disadvantage because it means that the world loses some of its linguistic variety. On the other hand, the information in Top Ten Languages mentions English as an international language, learned as a second or additional language by native speakers of other tongues. An advantage in a world tightly connected by electronic communication and transport is that people from widely different language groups and cultures can communicate easily with each other.

Vocabulary Building 1

Answer Key

A. **1.** characters; **2.** Linguists; **3.** language family; **4.** official language; **5.** mother tongue (or native/first language); **6.** native speaker; **7.** living language; **8.** dead language

B. Reading: reddened, dryness, brightness, quicken, lightness, saddened; Table: **2.** sadden, sadness; **3.** lighten, lightness; **4.** redden, redness; **5.** quicken, quickness; **6.** dryness

Teaching Notes

A. **Definitions:** Before attempting the definitions, have students use each term appropriately in a sentence for further practice. Then, have students do Activity A. Check answers as a class.

B. **Word Link:** Adding the suffix –en to certain adjectives turns them into verbs. If you add –ness to the same adjective, it becomes an abstract noun. Note that some consonants such as d double when the suffix is added. Have students complete the table before filling in the gaps in the paragraph in Activity B. Check answers as a class.

Challenge: Do you think Latin is a dead language? Answers may range from "Yes, because nobody speaks it in daily use" to "No, people still study it and it is used by historians and religious people."

Unit 4 Great Destinations

Unit Introduction

This unit focuses on famous travel landmarks, their history, and why they are popular with visitors.

Key Words for Internet Research: *Bollywood, Darjeeling Himalayan Railway, Elephanta, Gateway of India, Grand Central Terminal, Mumbai, national historic landmarks, Taj Mahal, Victoria Terminus*

For More Information: http://travel.nationalgeographic.com/places/

Warm Up

Answer Key

Answers will vary.

Teaching Notes

Write *Taj Mahal* on the board and pronounce it [tajzh mah hal]. Tell students to look at the photo and read the caption. Ask them:
- **In what country was this photo taken? In what city?** Agra, a city in northern India
- **What are the people in the photo doing?** They are guiding a steam train using arm motions and a flag. Steam trains have gone out of use in most countries now.
- **What is the building in the background?** The Taj Mahal, a famous tourist destination. It was originally built as a tomb or burial place by the ruler Shah Jahan.
- **Why do people visit the Taj Mahal?** It is an extremely beautiful monument, made from white marble with detailed carving and pieces of valuable colored stones. In the front is a reflecting pool, and in the back is a large garden. The Taj Mahal has a romantic story attached to it—Shah Jahan built it for his wife Mumtaz, whose name means *Wonderful Mahal*.

Lesson 4A Big City Travel

Lesson Overview

Target Vocabulary:

ceiling, conveniently, economic, feature, focal, located, modernization, object, sightseer, threaten

Reading Passage Summary:

Read about Manhattan's Grand Central Terminal and the successful fight to preserve it.

Answer Key

Before You Read

A. **1.** track; **2.** apartment; **3.** landmark; **4.** commuter; **5.** terminal
B. **1.** c; **2.** a; **3.** b; **4.** d

Reading Comprehension

A. **1.** b (lines 44–45); **2.** b (lines 29–32); **3.** c (paragraph 1 and caption to his photograph); **4.** a (line 19); **5.** b
B. **1.** information booth; **2.** newspaper (line 48); **3.** tobacco smoke; **4.** oldest business; **5.** Historic Landmark

Vocabulary Practice

A. **1.** located; **2.** threatened; **3.** modernizing; **4.** sightseers; **5.** economic
B. **1.** b; **2.** a; **3.** a; **4.** b; **5.** b

Teaching Notes

Before You Read

Before starting the exercises, have students look closely at the terrain map at the top half of page 52 as well as the street map on the right. Ask these questions:

- **What is the green area in the center?** Central Park
- **Why are the circles important?** They show landmarks described in the captions.
- **What are the buildings all around the edge of the park?** Apartment buildings
- **Where is Grand Central Terminal from Central Park?** A little to the south

A. Matching: Have students match the definitions with the highlighted words in Activity A. Check answers as a class.

B. Scan: Have students scan for numbers in the text to complete Activity B. All of the items can be answered from the fact file on page 54. Check answers as a class.

Reading Comprehension

A. Multiple Choice: Have students read the entire passage silently and answer the questions for Activity A. Check answers as a class, asking students to give evidence for their answers using line references from the passage. For Question 1, option "a" is by inference. If Grand Central is New York's largest terminal and New York is one of the world's largest cities, it must be true. Option "c" is found in lines 10–11, and option "d" is in lines 1–2. The answer "b" is found in the fact box on lines 44–45.

B. Completion: Have students complete Activity B, and then check answers as a class. The instruction to limit answers to a certain word limit is found in some standardized exams (e.g., IELTS), so check that students follow it.

Challenge: For students who have completed Activities A and B, write the following question on the board. Additional comprehension questions are available on the CD-ROM.

Can you find at least five secret places in the reading? What are they? (tennis courts, hidden railroad cars, a private apartment, the M-42 basement, and the hidden underground platform)

Vocabulary Practice

A. Completion: Have students do Activity A. Then, have students check answers with a partner.

B. Words in Context: Have students do Activity B. Check answers as a class.

Challenge: Have students who have completed Activities A and B use the maps on page 52 to figure out directions for a person walking from the Museum of Natural History to the Balto statue. Hint: use street names from the smaller map. Note that at http://grandcentralterminal.com/ students can explore the train terminal.

Word Partnership

The verb *locate* is usually paired with the prepositions *in* or *at*. For example, *Megan's office is <u>located in</u> an old house in the city center* or *My dentist's office is <u>located at</u> 41 North Street.* Common collocations with adverbs are *centrally located* and *conveniently located*.

Lesson 4B Postcards from India

Lesson Overview

Target Vocabulary: appeal (to), cave, cultural, derive, establish, permitted (to), policy, preserve, surrounding, supposedly

Reading Passage Summary: Take a short tour of Mumbai, India, and experience the city and some of its sights.

Answer Key

Before You Read

A. Photos are numbered clockwise from top left: 1 (snake charmers), 3 (Taj Mahal) and 2 (Kailash temple); **a.** diverse; **b.** impressive; **c.** monuments; and **d.** sculptures

B. a goddess

Reading Comprehension

A. 1. b; **2.** a (lines 21–22); **3.** c; **4.** b (lines 38–39); **5.** a

B. Colonial India: a, d, and f; Independent India: b and g; Both: c and e (still famous today)

Vocabulary Practice

A. a. cultural; **b.** derived; **c.** appeal; **d.** surround; **e.** established

B. 1. supposedly; **2.** permitted; **3.** cave; **4.** preservation; **5.** policies

Teaching Notes

Before You Read

A. Matching: The photo to the right shows people walking along the reflecting pool in front of the Taj Mahal. It is a *monument*, a large structure made of stone that is intended to remind people of the ruler's wife. The photo at the bottom shows a temple carved out of the stone surrounding it and there are smaller stone *sculptures* carved from stone in the front of the buildings.

B. Scan: Mumbai was named after the goddess Mumba who is also known as *Parvati*. The name *Bombay* came from the Portuguese *Bom Bahia*, meaning a good bay or harbor. Today Mumbai is one of the largest cities in the world. Although it has many prosperous neighborhoods and the famous Bollywood film production area, it also has a lot of poverty. One of the slums features in the Oscar-winning movie *Slumdog Millionaire*. In recent years, Mumbai has had a lot of violence, including the November 2008 attacks at some of the famous landmarks described in the reading.

Reading Comprehension

A. Multiple Choice: Have students read the entire passage silently and answer the questions for Activity A. Check answers as a class. Question 1 involves inference from paragraph 1 as well as using the process of elimination. Although it is true that Mumbai is home to Bollywood, the American film industry is based in Hollywood, California. Options "c" and "d" can't be correct because New York's colonial past was Dutch, not British.

B. Classification: Before having students do Activity B, ask them to read the passage at the top of page 61 that contains relevant information about Bollywood's founding date and the city's name. Note that India became independent from Britain in 1947. The Victoria Terminus became a World Heritage Site in 2004. For more information (including a 360° view) see http://whc.unesco.org/en/list/945/.

Challenge: For students who have completed Activities A and B, write the following question on the board. Additional comprehension questions are available on the CD-ROM.

Why would a visit to India give you sensory overload (page 58)? Explain.

Vocabulary Practice

A. Matching: Note the two phrasal verbs, *appeal to* and *derived from*. Have students do Activity A. Then, have students check answers with a partner.

B. Completion: Have students do Activity B. As students complete the sentences, ask them to pay attention to the part of speech needed for each gap. This will help them to use the correct form of words. Ask which of the vocabulary words on page 61 has a noun form (*culture, derivation, appeal, surround, establishment, permission, preservation,* and *policy*). Check answers as a class.

Challenge: For students who have completed Activities A and B, write the following question on the board. Additional vocabulary questions are available on the CD-ROM.

Have you ever seen a Bollywood film? Describe what it was like.

Word Partnership

A *policy* is a set of ideas, plans, or rules that are used as a basis for making decisions, especially in politics, economics, or business. Ask what policies students have to deal with. Examples might be absence policies or policies on dropping courses.

Explore More

Video Summary: The historic Darjeeling Himalayan Railway may be the slowest train in the world, but it is also one of the most beloved.

Answer Key

A. 1. a; **2.** a
B. 1. modernization; **2.** established; **3.** preserved;
   4. appeals; **5.** sightseers; **6.** surrounding;
   7. convenient; **8.** derive; **9.** permits; **10.** located

C. 1. It still works for travel in the mountains, and it appeals to tourists. **2.** Answers will vary.

Teaching Notes

A. Preview: For suggestions on building students' viewing skills, see pages 19–20. Have students look at the photo and read the caption. Ask students to complete Activity A. Elicit what students know about the name of the train. Write their ideas on the board and return to check them after viewing the video. Some ideas may be:

- Darjeeling is a famous tea growing area in the northeast of India.
- The Himalayas are a very high mountain chain. The train climbs over 2,000 meters on its journey.

See the photo gallery at the railroad's website http://www.dhrs.org/ to get a better idea of what the train and its mountainous route look like. The railway was built in the 1880s and became a World Heritage Site in 1999.

B. Summarize: Follow these steps:
1. Students watch the video through once, bearing in mind the answers they gave in the **Preview**.
2. Before playing the video a second time, ask students to read the summary and fill the gaps in Activity B with vocabulary items from the box. They close their books while watching the video.
3. After they've watched the video a second time, students complete or change their answers on the summary. Have them check answers with a partner.
4. If necessary, play the video through a third time and then check answers as a class.

C. Think About It: Have students answer the questions in Activity C in pairs. Discuss ideas as a class.

Unit Introduction

This unit focuses on severe storms, the damage they cause, and how people can prepare for them.

Key Words for Internet Research: *hurricane*, *Hurricane Katrina*, *natural disasters*, *New Orleans*, *severe storms*, *tornado*, *tropical cyclone*

For More Information: http://environment.nationalgeographic.com/environment/natural-disasters/hurricane-profile.html and http://environment.nationalgeographic.com/environment/natural-disasters/tornado-profile.html

Warm Up

Answer Key

1. Answers will vary. **2.** Storms can kill or injure people and animals; destroy homes; flood the land; and leave people without food, water, shelter, or electricity. **3.** Low-lying areas in Southeast Asia, Bangladesh, Myanmar, India, and China have had the greatest loss of life from storms. Severe storms also occur frequently along the Gulf of Mexico.

Teaching Notes

Tell students to look at the photo and read the caption. Ask them:
- **What kind of storm is this?** It is probably a hurricane with high tides and winds.
- **Where is Connecticut in the United States?** It is in New England in the northeast.
- **What is a sea wall?** It's a man-made structure of stone or concrete intended to protect property such as houses from ocean waves.

Storms range from mild rainstorms to severe weather events like hurricanes or tornadoes. Storms often have strong winds, thunder, lightening, and some form of *precipitation* such as rain, snow, or ice. *Hurricanes*—also known as *typhoons* and *cyclones*—start over warm water in tropical areas and are known for their strong winds and heavy rains. Weather scientists called *meteorologists* classify hurricanes by their wind strength on a scale from 1 to 5. Most deaths from hurricanes are caused by the *storm surge*, a powerful wall of water that happens when the storm first hits land. The storm surge can be six meters high and cover more than 150 kilometers. Once meteorologists know a storm is coming, they urge people to leave or *evacuate* the area so they are safe.

Many heavily populated places are in danger of flooding or storm surges because the land is so low. In some places, engineers have built strong stone or concrete walls to keep water out. These walls are called *levees*, *sea walls*, or *flood walls*. Such walls are mentioned throughout Unit 5A. There are pictures of them on pages 64, 66, and 68.

Lesson 5A   When Disaster Strikes

Lesson Overview

Target Vocabulary:

circumstance, currently, distribute, engineer, expose, ignore, resident, sector, sink, widespread

Reading Passage Summary:

Read about the cause of the flooding of New Orleans in 2005, the aftermath, and the city's future.

Answer Key

Before You Read

A. 1. helicopter; **2.** roof; **3.** flooding; **4.** levee
B. 1. Hurricane Katrina; **2.** Some people died or were injured, others lost homes and belongings.

Reading Comprehension

A. 1. d; **2.** c (line 6); **3.** d; **4.** b (line 46); **5.** d
B. a. 3; **b.** 4; **c.** 2; **d.** 5; **e.** 1

Vocabulary Practice

A. 1. exposed; **2.** ignore; **3.** circumstances; **4.** distributed; **5.** engineers; **6.** widespread; **7.** sectors; **8.** reside; **9.** sink
B. 1. sinking; **2.** resides; **3.** Circumstances; **4.** Engineers; **5.** exposed; **6.** ignore; **7.** distribute; **8.** widespread; **9.** sector

Teaching Notes

Before You Read

A. Matching: Direct students' attention to the concrete walls at the bottom left side of the photo on page 64. These are *levees*, designed to keep water out of the housing area. In New Orleans there are also levees to keep the Mississippi River within its banks (page 66). The levees broke and water got through. Have students do Activity A. Ask them about the flooding. How high do they think the water was? Why? Check answers as a class.

B. Discussion: Do students remember hearing about Hurricane Katrina on the news? It was a disaster for many reasons including the powerful storm, the damage to the city, the failure of people to leave when warned, and the complete breakdown of government that prevented help from coming through.

Reading Comprehension

A. Multiple Choice: Have students read the entire passage silently and answer the questions for Activity A. Check answers as a class, asking students to give evidence for their answers using line references from the passage. For Question 5, option "a" is not strictly true because the paragraph states that "some experts believe" and not the majority of people.

The models at the bottom of page 66 are part of the passage. They show what scientists predict will happen when hurricanes of different strengths hit New Orleans. The three maps show the same areas. Draw attention to the color-coded key for water depth. Ask students to describe how deep the water would be in each of the three circumstances.

B. Sequencing: Have students complete Activity B. Then, have students check answers as a class.

Challenge: For students who have completed Activities A and B, write the following question on the board. Additional comprehension questions are available on the CD-ROM.

If you lost your house and everything you owned during Hurricane Katrina, would you move back?

Vocabulary Practice

A. Completion: Have students do Activity A. Then, have students check answers with a partner.

B. Definitions: Have students use the words from the box above Activity A to complete the definitions. Check answers as a class.

Challenge: For students who have completed Activities A and B, write the following questions on the board. Additional vocabulary questions are available on the CD-ROM.
1. Name two things Dutch engineers have developed to cope with floods. (flood walls and floating houses)
2. Do you think these things would work in New Orleans? Why or why not?

Word Partnership

Ask the class to list some of the neighborhoods in their city on the board. What is special about each neighborhood?

Lesson 5B   Superstorm

Lesson Overview

Target Vocabulary:

blame, combination, cycle, energize, forecast, humid, professional, qualify, rotate, upward

Reading Passage Summary:

Find out how tropical cyclones (hurricanes or typhoons) are formed, their dangers, and difficulties in forecasting them.

Answer Key

Before You Read

A. 1. T; **2.** F; **3.** T; **4.** T

B. Students scan the passage to find the words in blue and check answers to Activity A.

Reading Comprehension

A. 1. c; **2.** d (footnote 2); **3.** b (line 17); **4.** a (line 32); **5.** b

B. 1. d; **2.** a; **3.** e; **4.** c; **5.** b

Vocabulary Practice

A. 1. humid; **2.** rotate; **3.** upward; **4.** qualifying; **5.** cycle; **6.** blame; **7.** forecast; **8.** professional; **9.** combination

B. 1. qualifies; **2.** blame; **3.** cycle; **4.** Professional; **5.** rotates; **6.** combination

Teaching Notes

Before You Read

A. True or False: Ask the class if they know the names of any major storms (e.g., Hurricanes Katrina, Firinga, Wilma 2005, Andrew 1992 in the United States; Cyclones Tracy 1974 in Australia, Nargis 2008 in Myanmar). Then, direct attention to the cyclone photo and caption at the top of page 69 and the world map. Remind students that the equator marks the divide between the northern and southern hemispheres. The map shows typical paths of cyclones and the months in which they are most likely to occur. Have students do Activity A. The questions can be answered from the photo, captions, and map. Check answers as a class.

B. Scan: Students now scan the main reading passage for the words in blue to check their answers.

Reading Comprehension

The passage has four main sections. The second section describes a chain of causes and events. Help students to understand the sequence by drawing a *chain graphic organizer* on the board and have them fill in each box.

A. Multiple Choice: Have students read the entire passage silently and answer the questions for Activity A. Check answers as a class. For Question 5, point out the difference between *rising sea levels*, something

that happens with global warming, and a *storm surge* in which sea levels rise suddenly and then fall again when the storm ends.

B. Matching: Have students do Activity B. Use of the graphic organizer and careful re-reading of paragraph 2 should help students with this task. Check answers as a class.

Challenge: For students who have completed Activities A and B, write the following questions on the board. Additional comprehension questions are available on the CD-ROM.
1. Do you think you can trust storm warnings and weather forecasts?
2. How accurate do you think weather forecasts are?

Vocabulary Practice

A. Completion: Have students read the passage silently and choose words from the box to fill the gaps in Activity A. They should pay attention to the words surrounding the gaps because most of the missing words occur in collocations such as *humid air*, *rotate around*, *upward from*, *qualifying as*, *repeating cycle*, *are to blame for*, and *combination of methods*. Check answers as a class.

B. Definitions: Have students do Activity B. Check answers as a class.

Challenge: For students who have completed Activities A and B, write the following question on the board. Additional vocabulary questions are available on the CD-ROM.

If people live in an area with severe storms, what can they do to prepare for them?

Explore More

Video Summary: The formation of Hurricane Katrina and how it developed into one of the most destructive storms in U.S. history is explained.

Answer Key

A. 1. catastrophic; **2.** destruction; **3.** tropical; **4.** condensation

B. 1. combination; **2.** circumstances; **3.** humid; **4.** upward; **5.** cycle; **6.** rotate; **7.** energized; **8.** qualified; **9.** exposed; **10.** widespread

C. 1. Some lessons learned are: be prepared for emergencies and have a plan; pay attention to weather forecasts and evacuate if told to; don't rebuild or live in areas that cannot be protected from storms.
2. Answers will vary.

Teaching Notes

A. Preview: For suggestions on building students' viewing skills, see pages 19–20. The video is about how Hurricane Katrina started as a tropical depression, became a tropical storm, and then enlarged through the hurricane categories. Have students complete Activity A and check answers as a class. Ask how the words could be applied to Hurricane Katrina and have students give examples. Some possibilities are:

- The situation was *catastrophic* because people couldn't get rescued.
- The *destruction* of neighborhoods was especially bad in low-lying areas.
- Hurricane Katrina was energized by heat from *tropical* waters.
- *Condensation* from hot air caused heavy rain to fall in New Orleans.

B. Summarize: Follow these steps:
1. Students watch the video through once, bearing in mind the answers they gave in the **Preview**.
2. Before playing the video a second time, ask students to read the summary and fill the gaps in Activity B with vocabulary items from the box. They close their books while watching the video.
3. After they've watched the video a second time, students complete or change their answers on the summary. Have them check answers with a partner.
4. If necessary, play the video through a third time and then check answers as a class.

C. Think About It: Have students answer the questions in Activity C in pairs. Discuss ideas as a class.

Unit Introduction

This unit focuses on coral reefs and sharks—learn about life within coral reefs and the threat they now face. Also read what scientists have learned about great white sharks.

Key Words for Internet Research: *coral reefs, cyanide fishing, great white shark, ocean ecosystems, ocean pollution, sharks, shark attack, shark tourism*

For More Information: http://environment.nationalgeographic.com/environment/habitats/canaries-of-sea.html and http://animals.nationalgeographic.com/animals/fish/great-white-shark.html

Warm Up

Answer Key

1. Answers will vary. **2.** Damage has been caused by numerous kinds of pollution, by over-fishing, and by physically hurting coral reefs and the ocean floor. In addition, global warming is having a negative effect on marine habitats. **3.** Some fish (barracuda, stonefish, lionfish, and scorpion fish), sharks, sting rays, and jellyfish are dangerous. Some kinds of coral sting as well.

Teaching Notes

Tell students to look at the photo and read the caption. Ask them:
- **What kind of fish is this?** It's an arrow blenny, a small bottom-dwelling fish that likes to hide in holes.
- **Where is the Caribbean Sea?** It is the body of water located south of the Gulf of Mexico, east of Central America, and north of South America. Find it on the map on page 76.
- **What is *prey*?** This fish is waiting for food or *prey* to swim by. It is a *predator*, an animal that hunts and kills others for food. In turn, it may be the *prey* for a larger animal.

The Pacific, Atlantic, and Indian Oceans cover about 71% of the Earth's surface. Have students locate these on the map on page 76.

Lesson 6A | Coral Reefs

Lesson Overview

Target Vocabulary:

brilliantly, conservation, consumption, creature, generation, jewelry, negative, pollution, shallow, source

Reading Passage Summary:

Read about coral reefs, their importance, and some of the threats they are facing.

Answer Key

Before You Read

A. 1. F; **2.** T; **3.** F; **4.** T
B. How coral is formed, Coral reef wildlife, and Problems affecting reefs

Reading Comprehension

A. 1. b; **2.** c (lines 14–15); **3.** b; **4.** c; **5.** b
B. 1. fish as possible; **2.** building material; **3.** liquid cyanide; **4.** the aquarium market; **5.** turn white

Vocabulary Practice

A. 1. conservation; **2.** shallow; **3.** creatures; **4.** negative; **5.** generations
B. 1. b; **2.** a; **3.** a; **4.** b; **5.** a

Teaching Notes

Before You Read

The Earth has several imaginary lines circling it. The equator divides the northern and southern hemispheres. The equator is at zero degrees latitude where the sun is directly overhead on March 21 and September 21. The Tropics of Cancer and Capricorn lie at 23.5 degrees latitude, respectively, north and south of the equator. They mark the northernmost and southernmost areas where the sun is directly overhead during the year. The area in between is called *the tropics* and it has less seasonal variation. Most coral reefs are found in the tropics because the waters there are consistently warm. Have students look at the equator, Tropic of Cancer, and Tropic of Capricorn on the map on page 76 and tell which countries the lines go through. Ask the class to name some places in the tropics.

A. True or False: Have students work in pairs to answer the questions from the map. Note that false statements need to be corrected. Check answers as a class.

B. Predict: Have students look at the headings, photos, and captions to predict what topics will be covered. Using cyanide is a health hazard to fishermen, but the topic is not covered in the passage.

Reading Comprehension

A. Multiple Choice: Have students read the entire passage silently and answer the questions for Activity A. Check answers as a class, asking students to give evidence for their answers using line references from the reading passage.

B. Completion: Have students complete Activity B. Then, have students check answers as a class. Remind students that their answers must be three words or less.

Challenge: For students who have completed Activities A and B, write the following questions on the board. Additional comprehension questions are available on the CD-ROM.

Do you know anyone who keeps an aquarium? Is this an easy hobby? Explain.

Vocabulary Practice

A. Completion: Have students do Activity A. Then, have students check answers with a partner.

B. Words in Context: Have students do Activity B. Check answers as a class.

Challenge: For students who have completed Activities A and B, write the following question on the board. Additional vocabulary questions are available on the CD-ROM.

How can countries protect their coral reefs? Give two examples.

Word Partnership

The adjective *negative* can be used to describe a fact, situation, or experience that is unpleasant, depressing, or harmful. Other common partnerships or collocations are a *negative impression* and a *negative reaction*.

Lesson Overview

Target Vocabulary:

arrange, bite, categorize, comprehend, confusion, factually, gather, horror, hypothesize, inaccurate

Reading Passage Summary:

Read about great white sharks, their attacks on people, and why so few people are actually eaten by them.

Answer Key

Before You Read

A. 1. a type of fish; **2.** length; **3.** teeth; **4.** dead things; **5.** nets

B. Some common ideas about sharks are not true.

Reading Comprehension

A. 1. c (lines 6–8); **2.** a (paragraph 2); **3.** b (line 26); **4.** c; **5.** b (line 25)

B. a. F (lines 28–29); **b.** T (lines 38–40); **c.** T (lines 41–43); **d.** F (lines 25–26); **e.** F (lines 31–33)

Vocabulary Practice

A. 1. horror; **2.** confusion; **3.** inaccurate; **4.** bite; **5.** factual

B. 1. comprehend; **2.** arranged; **3.** hypothesize; **4.** gather; **5.** categorized

Teaching Notes

Before You Read

Tell students to look at all the photos in the unit. Ask them:

- **What kind of shark is this mostly about?**
  Great white shark
- **How can researchers safely photograph sharks?** From inside diving cages

Sharks are fish that existed as long as 400 million years ago. Today there are about 400 species of sharks, but only four types attack humans—and not very often. Sharks have very flexible skeletons and a highly sensitive sense of smell. Sharks' teeth are constantly replaced during their lifetimes.

A. Completion: Have students do Activity A. Check answers as a class.

B. Predict: Students predict what the passage will be about from its title *The Truth About Sharks*.

Reading Comprehension

Draw students' attention to the key on the left side of the map. Note that the blue for range includes a large portion of the world's oceans, but the shades of purple and pink show where the great whites are usually found—in cool, coastal waters (not around the equator). Have students use the key to identify places where great white sharks can be found year-round. These would include the west coasts of North and South America, the south coasts of Africa and Australia, and the northeast coast of North America. Ask if great white sharks are found near places where your students live.

A. Multiple Choice: Have students read the entire passage silently and answer the questions for Activity A. Check answers as a class. Ask students to work in pairs to write a sentence about the main idea in each paragraph. Question 1 is as much about *sequence* as it is about detail. Ask students to tell the steps in Craig Rogers's story.

B. Fact or Theory: Point out that *T* and *F* here mean *theory* and *fact*, not *true* or *false*. Ask students to support their answers with line references from the passage.

Challenge: For students who have completed Activities A and B, write the following question on the board. Additional comprehension questions are available on the CD-ROM.

In the photo on page 83, why do you think the shark is attracted to the diving cage?

Vocabulary Practice

A. Completion: Have students do Activity A. They should pay attention to the words surrounding the gaps because some of the missing words occur in collocations such as *horror toward*, *confusion about*, and *factual information*. Check answers as a class.

B. Completion: Have students do Activity B. Check answers as a class.

Challenge: For students who have completed Activities A and B, write the following questions on the board. Additional vocabulary questions are available on the CD-ROM.

1. Do you think Peter Benchley was wrong to create such an inaccurate view of sharks?
2. Are authors of fiction required to be scientifically accurate? Explain.

Word Link

On page 80, *negative* was featured in the **Word Partnership** section. Another form of the word is the verb *negate* which means that one thing causes another thing to lose the effect or value that it had. That is what the prefix *in-* does to the meaning of words. Ask how the prefix *in-* affects these words: *inadequate*, *incapable*, *inconvenient*, *incorrect*, and *inhuman*. Have students use the words in sentences.

 # Explore More

Video Summary: Swimming with sharks may not be as scary as people think, but its increasing popularity raises questions about how safe it actually is.

Answer Key

A. 1. Answers will vary. **2.** Answers will vary. **3.** a
B. 1. creatures; **2.** horrified; **3.** negative; **4.** inaccurate; **5.** bite; **6.** hypothesize; **7.** confuse; **8.** consume; **9.** comprehends; **10.** factual
C. 1. Answers depend on the species or type of sharks (some are harmless to people) and whether the sharks are fed or not. **2.** Answers will vary. Some

ways of protecting marine environments include passing and enforcing laws prohibiting cyanide fishing or dragging nets across the ocean floor. Other ways include supporting organizations that attempt to educate people about the environment and endangered species.

Teaching Notes

A. Preview: For suggestions on building students' viewing skills, see pages 19–20. The video is about shark tourism where people get to scuba dive with sharks. In the past, some people fed sharks to attract them, but now the practice is criticized and illegal in some places. Some marine biologists believe that sharks learn to associate food with the presence of humans and feeding sharks increases the danger to tourists.

Have students complete Activity A. Although the first two questions ask for personal opinions, students may not have enough background knowledge on these topics to answer them before viewing the video. If this seems to be the case, return to the questions after the first viewing of the video. Ask students:

- What is scuba diving? What equipment and training do you need?
- What do scuba divers usually see beneath the surface?

- What positive things could people learn from diving with sharks?

B. Summarize: Follow these steps:
1. Students watch the video through once, bearing in mind the answers they gave in the **Preview**. Check back to see what responses students have to Questions 1 and 2 after viewing the video.
2. Before playing the video a second time, ask students to read the summary and fill the gaps in Activity B with vocabulary items from the box. They close their books while watching the video.
3. After they've watched the video a second time, students complete or change their answers on the summary. Have them check answers with a partner.
4. If necessary, play the video through a third time and then check answers as a class.

C. Think About It: Have students answer the questions in Activity C in pairs. Discuss ideas as a class.

Answer Key

A. Across: **1.** factual; **5.** object; **6.** located; **8.** cave; **11.** reside; **13.** preserve; **15.** exposed; **16.** source; **17.** bite; **18.** negative; **19.** surround

Down: **2.** convenient; **3.** rotate; **4.** permit; **7.** comprehend; **8.** cycle; **9.** creature; **10.** ignore; **12.** economic; **14.** sink

B. Australia, living things, 2,800, coral, fish, color, attach, 1975, garbage, pollution

Teaching Notes

A. Crossword: Before students attempt the crossword in Activity A, have them review the vocabulary from Units 4 through 6 using the **Target Vocabulary** list on pages 177–178 where words are given with unit numbers. Then, have students use the definitions to complete the crossword. They should fill in the words they know first, using letters as clues for more challenging items. Check answers as a class.

B. Notes Completion: Have students do Activity B. Check answers as a class.

World Heritage Spotlight: Great Barrier Reef

Background Information

Coral reefs can take many forms from *fringing reefs* attached to the land to *atolls*, circular coral structures that lie offshore. A *barrier reef* parallels the coastline, but it is separated from the land by a *lagoon*, an area of shallow salt water. Australia's Great Barrier Reef is the world's most outstanding example, but there are barrier reefs elsewhere such as off the coast of Belize in the Western Caribbean.

To protect the reef, Australia started a Biodiversity Action Plan (BAP). In this plan, marine biologists first survey the reef to get information about all the living things found there. They examine the status of each species to see if the population is healthy or endangered. Some species are found nowhere else on Earth, so it is very important to conserve them. Finally, they create a plan to protect and improve threatened parts of the reef while keeping other parts healthy. The reef's status as a World Heritage Site since 1981 has focused world attention on this natural treasure.

For More Information: http://video.nationalgeographic.com/video/player/science/earth-sci/oceans-barrier-reef.html and http://www.gbrmpa.gov.au/

Teaching Notes

Overview: The spread on pages 88–89 shows an aerial view plus several close-up views of the Great Barrier Reef.

Teaching Suggestions: This spread has three main text boxes. Divide the class into three groups and assign a box to each group. Each group has two tasks:

1. Write a sentence that describes what the box is mostly about. Samples are:
   a. This box describes the Great Barrier Reef, what it contains, how it works, and what visitors can see.
   b. This box gives some hypotheses about why fish in the Great Barrier Reef are so varied.
   c. This box tells about ways people are trying to protect the Great Barrier Reef.

2. Find some information in each box that is unusual or surprising.

Have a spokesperson for each group report to the rest of the class. Then, have everyone read the entire spread silently to prepare for a quiz you're going to give. Students stay in groups to answer the questions. The team with the highest number of correct answers wins. Have about 20 questions for the quiz. Here are some suggestions:

- **How long is the Great Barrier Reef?** 2,000 km (1,250 miles)
- **Give two examples of a mollusk.** Snails and squid
- **What does a wrasse [pronounced rass] do to other fish?** It cleans them by feeding on dead tissue, scales and parasites on their skin and mouths, which helps prevent infection and disease.
- **What does OUCH stand for?** Order of Underwater Coral Heroes
- **How much of the Great Barrier Reef is open to visitors?** Only 5%

- **Are algae plants or animals?** Plants
- **How big is a potato codfish?** As big as a full-grown man (refer to picture on page 89)
- **What's an *anchor*?** A heavy object that prevents a ship from moving
- **Did the Great Barrier Reef become a World Heritage Site later than Pompeii?** No. The Great Barrier Reef became a World Heritage Site in 1981, whereas Pompeii only became one in 1997 (refer to page 46).

Challenge: Unit 6A discussed many threats to coral reefs. Do you think the Great Barrier Reef suffers from these problems? Explain your answer.

A Global View: Water

Background Knowledge

To prepare students for the topic, ask some of these questions:

- Where do they get drinking water?
- How much water do they use each day? What for? Make a list on the board.

- In their country, what are the main sources for water?
- If applicable, how do farmers in their country water their crops?
- Where would you find glaciers today?

Teaching Notes

Overview: The spread on pages 90–91 deals with three topics about water: the circulation of water in the oceans, the world's supply of fresh water, and the water cycle. Water, especially access to clean, fresh water, is a major global issue, but students in some locations may not be aware that this is a problem because it doesn't affect their daily lives. It is useful to use specific examples of places where fresh water is scare to increase global awareness.

Key Words for Internet Research: *fresh water, water conservation, water crisis, water cycle, water scarcity*

For More Information: http://news.bbc.co.uk/2/hi/science/nature/3747724.stm and http://www.who.int/features/factfiles/water/en/

Building Graphic Literacy

Map Reading

The map on pages 90–91 shows the continents in black and the oceans in blue. The map shows the circulation of water in the oceans, and the map key is on page 91. Have students quickly scan the summary in the blue box on page 90 before focusing on the key. Ask what temperatures the colors refer to and find examples of each color. Point out that the lines represent moving *currents* of water and that the arrows show the direction in which they are moving. Point out the two symbols that indicate whether the water sinks or rises.

To illustrate the general idea, the warm current called the Gulf Stream moves north from an upwelling near South American into the Atlantic. As it approaches northern Canada and Greenland, a sinking occurs and the colder waters return south again. The importance of this is that the warm water makes places in the north warmer than they would be otherwise.

Find places with the "Sinking" symbol and ask students the following questions to check understanding:
- Are they near the equator?
- Are there any places with the "Upwelling" symbol near the equator?
- What do you think this means?

Pie Charts

Three pie charts or graphs are chained together to show the distribution of fresh water. In the first all-blue pie chart, it is easy to see that 97.5% of the water on Earth is salt water and only 2.5% is fresh water. The next pie chart focuses on where fresh water is located. Note that there are four categories to the second pie chart. The one that gets expanded into the final pie chart is surface and atmospheric water (at only 0.4%, less than half of 1%). The final pie chart shows that out of all surface and atmospheric water on Earth, 67.4% is in lakes, about 12.2% is in the soil, and the rest is in the atmosphere, wetlands, rivers, and *biota* (living things).

The main point of this series of pie charts is that of all the planet's water, only a tiny amount of fresh water is actually available for human use. Ask students the following questions to check understanding of the pie charts:
- **Which has more fresh water, glaciers or the ground?** Glaciers
- **Which holds more fresh water, rivers or lakes?** Lakes
- **Can salt water be used for daily activities?** The salt has to be taken out first, and the desalination process requires a lot of energy and expense.
- **What are some of the largest freshwater lakes?** The Great Lakes in North America and Baikal in Russia
- **Why not get more water from the ground?** That water has been there for millions of years. In many cases, once it is used up, it is gone forever.

Diagrams

The diagram on the top of page 91 shows the water cycle. Heat from the sun causes water to evaporate or rise as tiny moisture particles. In the atmosphere above the Earth, it cools and condenses to form moisture in clouds. The clouds release the moisture as precipitation in the form of rain or snow and it falls back to the Earth's surface. At that point, it fills lakes, rivers, and wetlands or it sinks into the soil. Most lakes and rivers eventually drain into the ocean and the process starts all over again. Ask students how the water cycle works in places they have lived in. Start with these questions:
- What form does precipitation take there?
- Are there any lakes or rivers? Do they become fuller at some times of year? When?
- Where do the rivers flow?
- Do you know of any underground sources of water?
- Are there any times of drought or periods without rain?

Word Link

The suffix *–(a)tion* changes some verbs to nouns that describe a process. Ask for examples other than those given on page 91. Some possibilities are: *transportation* and *accumulation*. Notice the core word *vapor* in *evaporation* that will help learners remember that the process involves turning liquid into a gas or minute water droplets.

Critical Thinking

In this unit, students think about ways to conserve the world's fresh water to meet the needs of people everywhere. Ask students these questions:
- Do you think that people in developed countries use more or less water than people in poorer countries?
- How can people who live where water is plentiful help people who live where water is scarce?
- What are some of the ways in which water is wasted today?
- If a farmer in Brazil uses chemical fertilizer, how could that affect water in India?

Vocabulary Building 2

Answer Key

A. 1. gulf; **2.** glacier; **3.** current; **4.** channel; **5.** poles;
6. tropics; **7.** clouds

B. Table: **2.** combination; **3.** condense; **4.** conservation;
5. distribute; **6.** evaporation; **7.** generate; **8.** location;
9. pollute; **10.** precipitation; **11.** preserve; **12.** rotation
Reading: evaporates, condenses, Precipitation,
circulation, distribution, pollution, Conservation/
preservation, generations

Note: *conservation*—saving and protecting the
environment—and *preservation*—keeping the situation
as it is—have very similar meanings. Either can be used
in the reading passage.

Teaching Notes

A. Definitions: Before attempting the definitions, have
students use each term appropriately in a sentence
for further practice. Then, have students do Activity A.
Check answers as a class.

B. Word Link: Students have additional practice
with the suffix *–(a)tion* as they fill in the chart
and complete the passage. Note that the words
distribution and *pollution* are different—both have a
suffix starting with *u* instead of *a*. In both cases, the
verb ends in *-ute*.

Challenge: Is there a connection between ocean
circulation and the water cycle? (There is some
connection since circulating currents have an effect on
temperature and moisture levels of nearby land. These
in turn affect temperatures, cloud cover, and types of
precipitation.)

Unit Introduction

This unit focuses on two industries that appeal to the sense of smell, the cut flower trade and perfume marketing.

Key Words for Internet Research: *cut flower industry, cut flowers, flower business, flower trade, perfume essences, perfume marketing, plants in Madagascar*

For More Information: http://www.flowers.org.uk/industry/industry-operation.htm
http://en.wikipedia.org/wiki/Perfume

Warm Up

Answer Key

A. 1. Answers will vary. Flowers have different names in each language, but also scientific botanical names in Latin. **2.** Answers will vary. *Scent* is the pleasant smell of a flower. **3.** People use flowers for decoration inside and outside their homes, for religious ceremonies, and for producing perfumes and medicines.

Teaching Notes

Write the words *kinkajou* and *balsa* on the board and pronounce them [kink ah joo, ball sah]. Tell students to look at the photo and read the caption. Ask them:
- **What is the animal in the photo doing?** It is drinking *nectar*, a sweet liquid in plant flowers.
- **What is a *kinkajou*?** A small, tropical mammal that lives in the rainforests of Central and South America. It eats a wide variety of foods including flowers, birds' eggs, and insects.
- **How do flowers benefit from animals/insects being attracted to them?** The plant produces pollen that sticks on to the animal/insect as they are feeding. The animal/insect then carries the pollen off to another flower and *pollinates* it. *Pollination* is how plants reproduce.

Lesson 7A The Business of Flowers

Lesson Overview

Target Vocabulary:

claim, considerable, dominate, employment, export, handle, prevent, purchase, renowned, trade

Reading Passage Summary:

The passage discusses recent changes in the cut flower trade including flower research, production of flowers in countries like Ecuador, auctions in the Netherlands, and shipping by air.

Answer Key

Before You Read

A. Students answer *yes* or *no* to complete the survey.
B. b. the international business of cut flowers

Reading Comprehension:

A. 1. c; **2.** b (lines 20–22); **3.** a; **4.** b (line 38); **5.** b (line 54)
B. 1. Netherlands: b and c; **2.** Ecuador: a and d;
   3. Both: e

Vocabulary Practice

A. 1. prevent; **2.** exported; **3.** trade; **4.** handle;
   5. purchased
B. 1. a; **2.** a; **3.** b; **4.** b; **5.** a

Teaching Notes

Before You Read

A. Survey: Students should work in pairs to explain their answers. The highlighted words *long-stemmed roses* and *orchids* are illustrated in the photographs. *Fragrance* means a good kind of smell or scent. A *vase* is a container for cut flowers.

B. Preview: Have students quickly read the title, photograph captions, and the first and last sentences of paragraphs to determine the main idea of the reading passage. Note that the globe maps and timeline on page 96 are part of the passage.

Reading Comprehension

A. Multiple Choice: Have students read the entire passage silently and answer the questions for Activity A. Check answers as a class, asking students to give evidence for their answers using line numbers from the reading passage.

Question 3 requires students to eliminate the items mentioned in the passage. Options B, C, and D are all covered in lines 22–25.

In Question 5, students must infer the meaning from the quote. It is not meant to be taken literally, so option "a" is wrong. Mr. Hale's statement referred to his family business and was mentioned in the context of cheaper imports, so option "b" is the best answer.

B. Classification: Remind students how Venn diagrams work. Each circle is for things that only fit under that heading, but the overlapping area is for characteristics that both groups share. Have students complete Activity B. Check answers as a class. Despite the photograph of tulips on page 95, most cut flowers in the Netherlands are grown in artificially heated and lighted greenhouses, so option "a" cannot be used for both categories.

Challenge: Write the following question on the board for students who have completed activities A and B. Additional comprehension questions are available on the CD-ROM.

Using the timeline on page 96, how long does it take for a rose growing on a Columbian mountain to reach the flower markets in U.S. cities?

Vocabulary Practice

A. Completion: Have students do Activity A. Ask students to work in pairs to circle the target words in the reading passage to notice how they are used. Then, ask students to check their answers with their partner.

Note that *export*—sending goods out of a country— is the opposite of *import*, introduced in Unit 3B. Most countries export items they produce and import those that they don't produce themselves. Ask students about exports and imports from their home countries.

B. Words in Context: Have students do Activity B. Check answers as a class. Then ask for an example sentence for each of the five words.

Challenge: Ask students who have completed activities A and B to talk quietly about possible disadvantages of the global cut flower business. Additional comprehension questions are available on the CD-ROM.
1. How would it affect our environment? (Huge amounts of fertilizers and pesticides are used to produce the flowers.)
2. Are they safe for workers to handle? Look at the woman in the photo on page 98. What is she wearing?

For more information, see http://news.bbc.co.uk/2/hi/science/nature/3498594.stm

---

Word Partnership

The verb *handle* as used in the reading passage means to deal with, manage, or trade in something, but it also means to touch something or move it with your hands. A visual example of the latter meaning is in the photographs on pages 94, 96, and 98 where workers are *handling* flowers. The Aalsmeer picture on page 95 shows the first meaning, that the auction house *handles* 19 million flowers a day.

Marketing Perfume

Lesson Overview

Target Vocabulary:

authority, budget, commercials, display, distinctly, emphasis, essence, guard, job, obtain

Reading Passage Summary:

The reading passage describes some of the ways the perfume industry markets products.

Answer Key

Before You Read

A. Answers will vary.
B. A new perfume for men was named for him. (lines 31–34)

Reading Comprehension:

A. 1. a; **2.** a (line 16); **3.** d (lines 21–23); **4.** a (lines 28–29); **5.** c
B. 1. b; **2.** d; **3.** c; **4.** e; **5.** a

Vocabulary Practice

A. 1. essences; **2.** obtained; **3.** distinct; **4.** budget; **5.** derived
B. 1. a; **2.** b; **3.** a; **4.** b; **5.** a

Teaching Notes

Before You Read

A. Discussion: *Hype* means a high level of publicity meant to publicize or promote a product. A unique bottle design or an eye-catching advertisement is one way of creating hype.

Ask students to brainstorm for descriptions of the perfume bottles and write the words on the board. Some possibilities are: *classic, modern, body-shaped, twisted, boxy, clear, opaque* (cloudy, opposite of transparent), *simple, masculine, feminine.* Ask for volunteers to help everyone understand what the words mean.

Continue the discussion in groups of four students. Have students point to specific perfume bottles as they answer Questions 1 and 2. Encourage students to support their opinions with reasons.

B. Scan: Michael Jordan made TV commercials and appeared on talk shows to create interest in the perfume named for him. Perfume advertisements often use celebrities to promote their products. Many celebrities like Britney Spears and David Beckham nowadays even have their own perfumes.

Reading Comprehension

A. Multiple Choice: Have students read the passage and complete Activity A. Check answers as a class.

For Question 3, have students look at the photos on pages 102 and 103 to realize that animal products as well as essences from plants and flowers are used for producing perfumes. Therefore, option "b" will not work because it only refers to plants and man-made essences. Option "d" is the best answer.

B. Matching: Students match headings with the main ideas of numbered paragraphs.

Challenge: Write the following questions on the board for students who have completed activities A and B. Additional comprehension questions are available on the CD-ROM.
1. What perfume products do you know or use that are named after famous people?
2. In the photo at the bottom of page 101, what are the people doing? Why? (Perfumes interact with a person's body chemistry, so they can only really be tested on a person's skin, not just by smelling a bottle.)

Vocabulary Practice

A. Completion: Have students do Activity A. Then have students work in pairs. They close their books and try to explain what *ambergris* is, using as many vocabulary words as possible.

Point out that in this reading *aroma* is used as a synonym for *smell*. What other synonyms do students know from this unit? (*scent, fragrance, perfume*) Are all of them positive? What are some negative words for smell? (*stink, stench, bad odor*)

B. Words in Context: Have students complete Activity B and check their answers with a partner. *Commercials* are a type of advertising on radio and TV. Other kinds of advertising include print ads in newspapers and magazines, electronic advertising on the Internet, and billboards.

Challenge: For students who have completed activities A and B, write the following question on the board. Additional vocabulary questions are available on the CD-ROM.

Where would you be likely to find a perfume commercial or advertisement? (Sometimes they appear on TV, but more often in magazines. Travelers see perfume advertisements in airline magazines because many travelers buy perfumes in duty-free shops.)

Word Partnership

The word *obtain* is a more formal form of the useful word *get*. Try substituting the word in the partnerships on page 103. The meaning is the same, but *get* is too informal for most combinations.

Explore More

Video Summary: Scientists are venturing deep into the forests of Madagascar to find exciting new scents and flavors for our products.

Answer Key

A. Answers will vary. **1.** Perhaps unusual floral scents; **2.** In perfumes, foods, and medicines
B. 1. exports; **2.** obtain; **3.** essences; **4.** distinctive; **5.** considerable; **6.** renowned; **7.** authority; **8.** joy; **9.** commercial; **10.** purchase

C. 1. Answers will vary.
2. Some possibilities are perfumes or personal care products such as deodorants, shampoo, and toothpaste.

Teaching Notes

A. Preview: For suggestions on building students' viewing skills, see pages 19–20. Have students look at the photo and read the caption. Ask students to complete Activity A. Brainstorm about what students know about Madagascar. Write students' ideas on the board and return to check them after viewing the video. Some ideas may be:
- Madagascar is an island off the east coast of Africa.
- Many unusual plants and animals are only found there. Lemurs are an example.
- Parts of Madagascar are very wild, so there may be unknown plants.

B. Summarize: Follow these steps:
1. Have students watch the video through once, bearing in mind the answers they gave in the **Preview**.

2. Before playing the video a second time, ask students to read the summary and fill the gaps in Activity B with vocabulary items from the box. They close their books while watching the video.
3. After they've watched the video a second time, students complete or change their answers on the summary. Have them check answers with a partner.
4. If necessary, play the video through a third time and then check answers as a class.

C. Think About It: Have students answer questions in Activity C in pairs. Discuss ideas as a class.

Unit 8 Great Explorers

Unit Introduction

This unit focuses on famous explorers and their travels: Marco Polo, Ibn Battuta, and the Arnesen-Bancroft team.

Key Words for Internet Research: *Arnesen and Bancroft*, *famous expeditions*, *famous journeys*, *great explorers*, *Ibn Battuta*, *Kubla Khan*, *Marco Polo*

For More Information: http://library.thinkquest.org/C001692/

Warm Up

Answer Key

A. 1. Answers will vary. Some famous explorers are Marco Polo, Ferdinand Magellan, and Zheng He. **2.** The ocean floor remains to be explored in many places, as well as the remote interiors of Amazon rainforests and Indonesian jungles. **3.** Answers will vary, but expect reasons for the response.

Teaching Notes

Write the words *Sahara*, *Tuareg*, and *nomad* on the board and pronounce them [Sah **hahr** rah, **Twah** reg, **no** madd]. Tell students to look at the photo and read the caption. Ask them:

- **What is the person in the photo doing?** Walking across a sand dune
- **What is the sand dune part of?** The Sahara Desert in North Africa
- **What group does the person belong to?** He is a member of the *Tuareg*, a nomadic group that moves back and forth across the Sahara with trade caravans and animals. See Unit 9B.
- **What is a guide?** Someone who knows an area well and can help other people travel there

Lesson 8A Marco Polo

Lesson Overview

Target Vocabulary:

administration, admire, contribution, journal, mineral, objective, palace, perceive, undertaking, voyage

Reading Passage Summary:

The passage describes Marco Polo's long journey, his service to Kublai Khan, and technologies he learned about in the East.

Answer Key

Before You Read

A. 1. Venice, 24; **2.** Locations in China from Shangdu in the north, all along the coast to Quanzhou in the south, then into Southeast Asia; **3.** Other places he visited include Istanbul, Jerusalem, Beijing, and Xi'an.

B. 1. To meet the powerful Mongol leader, Kublai Khan and work for him

Reading Comprehension:

A. 1. d; **2.** b (lines 23–24); **3.** b (lines 27–28); **4.** d; **5.** c (line 41)

B. 1. 1266:3; **2.** 1271:2; **3.** 1275:1; **4.** 1292:5; **5.** 1299:4

Vocabulary Practice

A. 1. voyage; **2.** objective; **3.** administration; **4.** contributed; **5.** journal; **6.** perceived; **7.** undertook; **8.** admire; **9.** Palace

B. 1. undertake; **2.** voyage; **3.** admire; **4.** perceive; **5.** palace; **6.** Administration; **7.** objective; **8.** journal; **9.** contribute

Teaching Notes

Before You Read

A. Discussion: Direct students' attention to the map and the note in the lower left corner. Place names change over time and the current name comes first on this map. Point out how Marco Polo's route can be traced by looking at the directions of the arrows.

B. Predict: The first paragraph of the reading passage contains the word *objective*, a goal someone is trying to achieve. Have students skim the second paragraph to find out why the meeting was long awaited (Marco Polo's father and uncle had already met Kublai Khan on an earlier visit).

Reading Comprehension

A. Multiple Choice: Have students read the entire passage silently and answer the questions for Activity A. Check answers as a class, asking students to give evidence for their answers using line numbers from the reading passage.

Question 1 has a format often used in examinations, the "all-of-the-above" response. Encourage students to read all the options before choosing the right answer. In this case, options "a–c" are individually correct, but the best answer is "d" that includes all of them.

Question 4 requires students to infer whether the East or West first had asbestos cloth, paper money, and coal. Key points are in line 31: ". . . not yet in use in the West . . ." and lines 33–34: "unknown in most of Europe."

B. Sequencing: Students have to match dates with events. Encourage students to read all the events before starting. Ask them to circle all the dates in the reading and on the map before doing the exercise. The 1266 date is obtained by subtracting five years from the starting date of 1271 on the map.

Challenge: Write the following questions on the board for students who have completed Activities A and B. Additional comprehension questions are available on the CD-ROM.
1. How long did the return journey take? (three years from 1292 to 1295)
2. What other famous explorer was influenced by Marco Polo? (Columbus, see ***Did You Know?***)

Vocabulary Practice

A. Completion: Have students do Activity A. Ask students to work in pairs to circle the target words (those in red) in the reading passage on pages 107 and 108 to notice how they are used. Then, ask students to check their answers with their partner.

B. Definitions: Have students do Activity B. Check answers as a class. Write the word *perception* on the board and ask which word it is related to (perceive). What was Polo's perception of Kublai Khan?

Note that *mineral* is not used in either activity. Ask the class for examples of minerals.

Challenge: Ask students who have finished Activities A and B to talk quietly about whether they think Marco Polo's journal was accurate. What recent developments could they mention to support their opinions?

Word Partnership

When someone *undertakes* a task or project, he or she commits to it and promises to do it. Other common combinations include: *undertake a journey*, *undertake an assignment* (especially in journalism such as the one mentioned on page 110 by *National Geographic* photographer Michael Yamashita), or in some World Heritage Sites, *undertake a reconstruction* of a place that has been ruined or damaged.

Lesson Overview

Target Vocabulary:

consent, finance, misfortune, prior, profitable, remote, translate, unparalleled, unpredictable, wisdom

Reading Passage Summary:

The reading passage describes some of the adventures of Ibn Battuta as he traveled widely throughout Asia and Africa in the 14th century.

Answer Key

Before You Read

A. 1. Islam; **2.** Ibn Battuta; **3.** the equivalent of 44 modern countries (refer to line 11 in the passage); **4.** 30
B. Students scan to check answers.

Reading Comprehension:

A. 1. b; **2.** a (line 8); **3.** c (lines 25–26);
    4. d (lines 12–14); **5.** d (lines 33–35)
B. 1. NG; **2.** T (line 12); **3.** T (line 22); **4.** F (lines 27–28);
    5. NG

Vocabulary Practice

A. 1. remote; **2.** prior; **3.** unparalleled; **4.** profitable;
    5. misfortune
B. 1. translators; **2.** unpredictable; **3.** financed;
    4. consented; **5.** wisdom

Teaching Notes

Before You Read

Ibn Battuta started his journey with a pilgrimage to Mecca on the Arabian Peninsula, one of the five main beliefs in Islam. Every Moslem is supposed to make the pilgrimage to Mecca if they possibly can. The photograph on page 112 shows pilgrims at this holy place. Ibn Battuta studied law and religion in Mecca for several years before continuing his travels.

A. Discussion: All questions except 3 can be answered by looking at information on the map.

B. Scan: Remind students that they *scan* for specific information. Review the word *decade* (line 9) that means a ten-year period.

Reading Comprehension

A. Multiple Choice: Have students read the passage and complete Activity A. Check answers as a class.

For Question 4, students need to determine which statement reflects the author's views most closely. The key is in lines 12–14 where the writer regrets that Ibn Battuta is not well known in the West.

B. True or False: Students decide whether the statements are *true*, *false*, or *not given* in the passage. The NG option requires students to read the passage very carefully and not just leap to conclusions based on partial information. For statement 1, students could confuse *birthplace* with *birthday* in line 1. For statement 5, there is only mention of one child in line 32.

Challenge: Ask students to compare the lives of Marco Polo and Ibn Battuta. Name at least three things they had in common (both lived to return home, both were in the service of rulers who lived in luxurious palaces, both wrote books about their travels).

Vocabulary Practice

A. Completion: Ask students to work with a partner. For each word they use to fill the gap, have them think of a synonym or phrase that gives the general meaning. Some examples are: (1) distant, far-away, hard-to-reach; (2) previous, earlier; (3) unmatched; (4) money-making; (5). bad luck.

B. Completion: Ask students to identify clues in each sentence that helped them select the best word.

Challenge: For early finishers, write the following question on the board. Additional vocabulary questions are available on the CD-ROM.

Do you think that Ibn Battuta generally had good luck or misfortune in his life? Give some examples.

Thesaurus

Students may be familiar with other meanings of the word *remote*. Ask them about how these examples are related to the meaning given on page 115: *TV remote control*, *a remote chance* (of something happening), *a remote ex-girlfriend*.

 ## Explore More

Video Summary: Two determined women talk about what inspired them to ski across Antarctica, and how they shared their story with the world.

Answer Key

A. b. on skis.
B. 1. contribution; **2.** remote; **3.** unparalleled;
4. perceive; **5.** voyage; **6.** Prior; **7.** unpredictable;
8. misfortunes; **9.** journal; **10.** financed or admired

C. 1. extreme cold, having to carry all supplies with them, trying to communicate from Antarctica
2. Answers will vary. For ideas, see http://adventure.nationalgeographic.com/

Teaching Notes

A. Preview: For suggestions on building students' viewing skills, see pages 19–20. Have students look at the photo and read the caption. Ask students to complete Activity A. Brainstorm about what students know about Antarctica. Write students' ideas on the board and return to check them after viewing the video. Some ideas may be:

- It is the fifth largest and the coldest continent. About 98% of it is covered by ice.
- It does not belong to any one country although several countries have research stations there. No one lives there permanently.
- It includes the South Pole that was not explored until 1911.
- It has many high mountains.

Arneson and Bancroft, both former school teachers, believe it is important to attempt expeditions as role models to young people, especially women. Although Arnesen and Bancroft were successful in crossing Antarctica on skis, some of their recent attempts to repeat their feat in the Arctic have met with misfortune. In 2005, their trip was cancelled because they couldn't get political permission for some areas. In 2008, Arnesen developed frostbite in a toe, and they had problems with electronic equipment malfunctioning in the cold. For more about their adventures and journeys, see http://www.nationalgeographic.com/adventure/news/liv-arnesen-frostbite.html.

B. Summarize: Follow these steps:
1. Have students watch the video through once, bearing in mind the answers they gave in the **Preview**.
2. Before playing the video a second time, ask students to read the summary and fill the gaps in Activity B with vocabulary items from the box. They close their books while watching the video.
3. After they've watched the video a second time, students complete or change their answers on the summary. Have them check answers with a partner.
4. If necessary, play the video through a third time and then check answers as a class.

C. Think About It: Have students answer questions in Activity C in pairs. Discuss ideas as a class.

Unit 9 | Traditions and Rituals

Unit Introduction

This unit introduces the Japanese traditional sport of sumo wrestling and describes a wedding ritual among the Tuareg people of the Sahara.

Key Words for Internet Research: *Day of the Dead in Mexico, Nubian wedding, sumo wrestling, the Tuareg wedding, Wodaabe*

For More Information: http://channel.nationalgeographic.com/series/explorer/3102/Videos/06083_00#tab-Overview

Warm Up

Answer Key

Answers will vary for all three questions.

Teaching Notes

Tell students to look at the photo and read the caption. Ask them:
- **What is happening in the photo?** People are gathered together to celebrate the Day of the Dead in Mexico.
- **What is the Day of the Dead?** In South America, people go to cemeteries on November 1 and 2 to pray for people who have died and to remember them. They believe the spirits of the dead will return on those days for a reunion with their families.
- **What happens in this tradition?** People bring food, sweets, and drinks to the cemetery as well as photos, candles, flowers, and even toys for children who died.

A *tradition* is a custom or belief that has existed for a long time and is often handed down from generation to generation. A *ritual* is a religious service or other ceremony with a series of actions performed in a fixed order.

Lesson 9A | A Sporting Ritual

Lesson Overview

Target Vocabulary:

dimension, grip, hero, illustrate, impact, internationalize, origin, pure, restriction, shame

Reading Passage Summary:

Read about the Japanese sport of sumo wrestling, its connections with ancient traditions, and the involvement of foreign fighters in the sport.

Answer Key

Before You Read

A. From top to bottom: 4, 1, 3, 2
B. 1. stare at each other, slap, push, trip, and grip the other wrestler's belt (lines 2–3); **2.** silk (line 19); **3.** samurai (line 20); **4.** 4.55 meters across (line 23)

Reading Comprehension

A. 1. a (lines 7–8); **2.** b (line 11); **3.** d (line 4); **4.** a (line 24); **5.** b (paragraphs 5 and 6)
B. Paragraph 1. b; **Paragraph 2.** e; **Paragraph 3.** d; **Paragraph 4.** a; **Paragraph 5.** c

Vocabulary Practice

A. 1. internationalization; **2.** grip; **3.** origin; **4.** restricted; **5.** shame
B. 1. a; **2.** a; **3.** b; **4.** a; **5.** a

Teaching Notes

Before You Read

Write the words *sumo wrestler* on the board and pronounce them [**sue** mow **ress** ler] noting that the *w* of wrestler is silent. Have students look at the photos and read the captions before starting the labeling. Ask the class to comment on the photos and draw their attention to the power and force shown in the photos on top of pages 118–119. Ask if they have ever seen sumo wrestling on TV. If so, ask them to describe it.

A. Labeling: Students read the sentences that describe various aspects of sumo wrestling and then label the arrows on the picture in Activity A. Check answers as a class.

B. Scan: Have students do Activity B. Then check answers as a class, asking students to give evidence for their answers using line references from the passage.

Reading Comprehension

As seen in the photos on the bottom of pages 119–120, sumo wrestlers are required to live in training schools run by retired sumo champions. Life in these schools is strictly controlled by tradition. Boys enter the school at about age 15 and gradually work their way up through a system of ranks as they become better fighters. Even the champions must live according to the restrictions about practice, dress, food, and sleep in these schools. For more about sumo wrestling and its events, go to http://www.sumo.or.jp/eng/.

A. Multiple Choice: Have students read the entire passage silently and answer the questions for Activity A. Check answers as a class, asking students to give evidence for their answers using line references from the passage.

B. Matching: Have students complete Activity B, and then check answers as a class. Have students work in small groups to say why they think headings fit the paragraphs.

Challenge: For students who have completed Activities A and B, write the following question on the board. Additional comprehension questions are available on the CD-ROM.

What are two ways sumo wrestling is connected to the Shinto religion? (Answers can be found in lines 25–28.)

Vocabulary Practice

A. Completion: Have students do Activity A. Then, have students check answers with a partner.

B. Words in Context: Have students do Activity B. Check answers as a class.

Challenge: For students who have completed Activities A and B, write the following question on the board. Additional vocabulary questions are available on the CD-ROM.

Using text and photos, describe three examples of Japanese traditional dress in this chapter.

Word Partnership

Impact can be a verb, adjective, or noun. Meteors do not *impact* Earth very often. The *impact* crater caused by the meteor is huge. The crater has had a positive *impact* on tourism in the area.

Lesson 9B Marriage Traditions

Lesson Overview

Target Vocabulary:

camp, demonstrate, jealous, nearby, reserve, reunite, symbol, tent, wedding, wrap

Reading Passage Summary:

Read about the wedding ceremony of a young Tuareg couple who live near the Sahara Desert.

Answer Key

Before You Read

A. Similar: all are ceremonies marking a change of status, the participants wear special clothes, all of the brides have some covering in or on their hair; Different: the colors of the clothes are different as are the specific rituals and traditions.

B. b. A traditional wedding

Reading Comprehension

A. 1. d; **2.** a (lines 21–22); **3.** d (lines 39–41); **4.** b (lines 44–47); **5.** c (line 58)

B. 1. b; **2.** e; **3.** d; **4.** a; **5.** c

Vocabulary Practice

A. 1. tents; **2.** camp; **3.** reserved; **4.** symbol; **5.** demonstrates; **6.** wrapped; **7.** reunite; **8.** weddings

B. 1. symbol; **2.** reserved; **3.** tent; **4.** wrap; **5.** wedding; **6.** reunited; **7.** demonstrate; **8.** camp

Teaching Notes

Before You Read

Ask about the locations mentioned in the captions. Kodiak Island is in the Aleutian chain southwest of Alaska, and the people pictured are probably native Aleuts. In Venice, a city of canals, traveling in a boat called a *gondola* is quite common. In Rajasthan in northwest India, grooms dressed in white ride white horses to their wedding ceremony, and marriages are still arranged by the couple's families.

A. Discussion: Students find similarities and differences in the three wedding examples.

B. Skim for the Main Idea: Have students do Activity B. Check answers as a class.

Reading Comprehension

The Tuareg were traditionally nomads and animal herders. Tuareg traders led caravans of camels across the Sahara Desert. The picture of the unmarried woman on page 125 shows an indigo cloth similar to the one worn by Tuareg men. The indigo dye rubs off easily and has led to the group being called the *Blue People*.

Today, some Tuareg have settled in the *Sahel*, the savannah area of grasslands and acacia trees south of the Sahara. See http://video.nationalgeographic.com/video/player/places/index.html for two videos of present-day Tuareg living in Mali.

A. Multiple Choice: Have students read the entire passage silently and answer the questions for Activity A. Check answers as a class, asking students to give evidence for their answers using line references from the passage.

B. Matching: Have students do Activity B. Check answers as a class.

Challenge: For students who have completed Activities A and B, write the following question on the board. Additional comprehension questions are available on the CD-ROM.

Describe the sequence of events in a Tuareg wedding. How long does it last? Who participates in the celebration?

Vocabulary Practice

A. Completion: Have students do Activity A. Then, have students check answers with a partner.

B. Completion: Have students do Activity B. Check answers as a class.

Note: Neither *jealous* nor *nearby* is used in the exercises. Have students use the words in sentences to check that they understand them. Ask about *jealousy* and what causes it.

Challenge: For students who have completed Activities A and B, write the following question on the board. Additional vocabulary questions are available on the CD-ROM.

Although the Tuareg and the Wodaabe are both nomadic African people, there are differences in their approach to marriage. Describe some things that are different. Are there any similarities?

Word Link

Re- is a prefix that means that something is happening again. Write the following words on the board and ask what is repeated: *reappear, rearrange, reconsider, reconstruct, recount, recreate, refuel, relocate, renew, repay, rethink*

Explore More

Video Summary: Learn more about wedding customs of the Nubian people in Egypt and how they play an important role in maintaining endangered traditions.

Answer Key

A. 1. c; **2.** a; **3.** d; **4.** b

B. 1. wedding; **2.** reunited; **3.** symbol; **4.** purity; **5.** original; **6.** restricted; **7.** impact; **8.** wrapped; **9.** grips; **10.** nearby

C. 1. Using incense and henna, wearing gold jewelry, having week-long wedding celebrations
2. Answers will vary.

Teaching Notes

A. Preview: For suggestions on building students' viewing skills, see pages 19–20. The video is about a wedding in another African group, the Nubians. Four thousand years ago, the Nubians had a great civilization along the Nile River. In recent times, Nubians were forced to move when the Aswan Dam was built. Ceremonies like weddings are important in maintaining their cultural traditions.

Have students complete Activity A and then check answers as a class. The purpose is to familiarize students with words they will hear in the video. Ask them:

- What kinds of *drums* do you know? How are they played?
- Are *swords* used in your culture? When and how?
- What does *incense* smell like? Why do people use it?

B. Summarize: Follow these steps:
1. Have students watch the video through once, bearing in mind the answers they gave in the **Preview**.
2. Check back to see what responses students have to Questions 1 and 2 after viewing the video.
3. Before playing the video a second time, ask students to read the summary and fill the gaps in Activity B with vocabulary items from the box. They close their books while watching the video.
4. After they've watched the video a second time, students complete or change their answers on the summary. Have them check answers with a partner.
5. If necessary, play the video through a third time and then check answers as a class.

C. Think About It: Have students answer the questions in Activity C in pairs. Discuss ideas as a class.

Answer Key

A. Across: 1. symbol; **5.** pure; **6.** impact; **7.** obtain; **9.** grip; **10.** jealous; **12.** unparalleled; **15.** purchase; **16.** display; **17.** remote; **18.** budget

Down: **1.** shame; **2.** finance; **3.** prevent; **4.** misfortune; **8.** voyage; **9.** guard; **11.** admire; **13.** nearby; **14.** export

B. Mali, Sahara Desert, commerce, 2,000, mud bricks, masons, Mosque, gold, ancient books

Teaching Notes

A. Crossword: Before students attempt the crossword in Activity A, have them review the vocabulary from Units 7 through 9 using the **Target Vocabulary** list on pages 177–178 where words are given with lesson numbers. Then, have students use the definitions to complete the crossword. They should fill in the words they know first, using letters as clues for more challenging items. Check answers as a class.

B. Notes Completion: Have students do Activity B. Check answers as a class.

World Heritage Spotlight: Old Towns of Djénné and Timbuktu

Background Information

Djénné and Timbuktu are both located in northern Mali at a place where the Niger River annually floods into lakes and swamps. Because of the natural irrigation from the river, people live by farming, fishing, and raising animals in this arid region. In the past, the mud cities were famous for gold and salt traded across the Sahara Desert. Islam followed the trade routes, and Djénné and Timbuktu became renowned centers of religious scholarship. Medieval explorers Ibn Battuta and Leo Africanus visited the cities and wrote about what they saw there. The cities prospered until the late 1500s when the Portuguese developed a competitive sea trade with cities on the West African coast.

The Grand Mosque in Djénné, pictured on page 131, is the largest mud brick building in the world. Originally built in the 13th century, it was restored by the French in 1907. However, the yearly rains harm mud buildings so they need regular repair. In Djénné, this maintenance is part of an annual festival involving special food and music in addition to skilled masonry.

Despite the annual repairs, Djénné and Timbuktu are threatened because of *desertification*, the spread of the Sahara Desert. The blowing sands and dry wind are unstoppable. For this reason, the World Heritage Organization listed Timbuktu as an endangered site in 1990 and UNESCO is now working to conserve the mud cities.

For More Information: See http://ngm. nationalgeographic.com/ngm/0106/feature6/fulltext. html for an article on Djénné. See http://whc.unesco. org/en/list/119 for Timbuktu.

Teaching Notes

Overview: The main pictures on pages 130–131 show traders resting by the river, with their horse-drawn carts bearing goods destined for the West African markets. The other photographs show young masons in Djénné, the famous mud homes of Timbuktu, and Djénné's Great Mosque. There is a glossary for terms that appear in bold.

Teaching Suggestions: The spread on pages 130–131 has three main text boxes. Divide the class into three groups and assign a box to each group. Each group has two tasks:

1. Write a sentence that describes what the box is mostly about. Samples sentences include:
   a. This box describes the historical mud cities of Djénné and Timbuktu and how they are maintained.
   b. This box tells about the connection of Djénné with Islam.

c. This box tells about Timbuktu as a trading and religious center.

2. Find some information in each box that is unusual or surprising. Have a spokesperson for each group report to the rest of the class. Then, have everyone read the entire spread to prepare for a quiz. Students stay in groups to prepare ten questions about details. Pool all the questions together and, taking turns, ask each group a question. The group has five seconds to answer. If the question is not answered correctly in that time, ask the next group. The group with the most correct answers wins. Here are some suggestions for questions:

   • **In what country are Djénné and Timbuktu located?** Mali
   • **What work are the boys in the photo doing?** Carrying mud for the masons to repair the buildings

   • **What is a mosque? When was the one in Djénné built?** A place for Muslims to worship. 13th century.
   • **What goods were traded? Why were they profitable?** Gold and salt. Gold is rare and salt essential for health and preserving food. There are not many sources for salt.
   • **How many old books are in the collection at Timbuktu?** 100,000
   • **When did Ibn Battuta visit Timbuktu?** 1352
   • **What shape are the mud houses?** Square or rectangular
   • **What does *exotic* mean?** Unusual and interesting
   • **When did the mud cities become World Heritage Sites?** 1988

   Challenge: Why would someone want to visit Djénné or Timbuktu today? Explain your answer.

A Global View: Trade

Background Knowledge

To prepare students for the topic, ask some of the following questions about their belongings:

   • What countries do your clothes and shoes come from?
   • How much of the food you eat is produced nearby? Imported?

   • If you contact a service center, for example, a computer service center, who helps you—and where is that person based?

Teaching Notes

Overview: Pages 132–133 deal with international trade, the exchange of consumer goods, machinery, raw materials (oil, uranium), capital (money for investment), services, and food. *Free trade* means there are few government restrictions and it is easy to trade with other countries. The opposite is *protectionism*, where countries restrict trade by using taxes and quotas to protect national interests.

Globalization means the increasing integration of societies and economies throughout the world, so that people, money, and capital move more easily across borders.

Fair trade is a social movement to make sure that producers (usually in developing countries) benefit from trade with decent social and environmental conditions that make their work sustainable. This often applies to agricultural products such as coffee, fruit, and flowers (see Unit 7A).

Key Words for Internet Research: *fair trade, free trade, globalization, international trade, World Trade Organization*

For More Information: Visit http://en.wikipedia.org/wiki/Imports for international trade. See http://www.pbs.org/illicit/ for a National Geographic documentary on illicit trade.

Building Visual Literacy

Map Reading

The upper map on page 132 displays information about the importance of international tourism to countries throughout the world. For many countries, the money tourists spend on services such as hotels, food, sight-seeing, and transportation is a significant part of their economy.

Draw attention to the map key that uses shades of blue to indicate the number of tourist arrivals in thousands per year. Therefore, the top category of "more than 40,000" really means 40,000,000 or 40 million tourists per year. Go through the key with students to find what happens when three "0"s are added to each number. Note too that the scale is very uneven. For example, the second category covers a much wider range than do those beneath it. Ask students the following questions to check comprehension:

- **Name a large area which has minimal tourism.** The sub-Sahara area of Africa which includes Djénné and Timbuktu.
- **Why do you think this situation exists?** It is remote and impoverished.
- **What are some places that lack data about tourism?** Greenland and Central Asia, both difficult places for tourists to travel to.

Reading Map Diagrams

The lower map on pages 132–133 shows the flow of trade between different parts of the world. Note that only continents are identified, not specific countries, and not all continents are included since no trade flow is shown in or out of Australia.

The key contains arrows of different colors to indicate the amount of trade in billions of U.S. dollars. Note the colors, width, and direction of the arrows differ. Ask for examples of the lowest two categories. (Trade between South America and the Middle East is an example of the lowest category.)

In using the map diagram, encourage students to actively use the highlighted vocabulary from the spread such as *producer/consumer* and *import/export*. Ask students the following questions to check comprehension:

- **What is South America's biggest trade partner?** North America
- **Describe the flow of trade between Europe and North America.** Europe exports more than it imports.
- **What kinds of things are produced in Asia and consumed in Europe and North America?** Consumer goods like electronics and manufactured goods for Walmart
- **What is exported from the Middle East and where does it go?** Oil. It goes everywhere!

Reading Bar Graphs

The bar graphs on the right side of page 133 measure countries by amounts. Although both graphs measure in billions of U.S. dollars, the top graph goes only to $800 billion while the bottom one extends to $1,200 billion. Note that the order of countries is different for exports and imports although the same ten countries are measured. Ask students the following questions to check comprehension:

- **What are the top three exporting countries?** United States, Germany, China
- **What are the top three importing countries?** United States, China, Germany
- **Compare exports and imports for the United States. Is there a balance, a deficit, or a surplus?** A deficit
- **Can you name at least two countries with a trade surplus?** China, Germany, United Kingdom, Japan

Vocabulary in Context

In this Global View, some new vocabulary is defined in parentheses. Ask the class about *producers*, *consumers*, *goods*, *services*, and *tourism services*.

Word Link

The suffix *-ism* changes some verbs to abstract nouns that often describe a system of beliefs. Write the following words on the board and ask the class to say what they mean: *heroism, activism, optimism, feminism, terrorism, patriotism, realism* (in art and literature), and *criticism*.

Critical Thinking

Have students think about how their own country fits into the global flow of trade. Ask them:

- Does your country export manufactured goods, raw materials, or services?
- What does your country import and why?
- What are your country's main trade partners? Do they import or export things?
- Do you think your country has a trade deficit, surplus, or balance? Find out and report to the class.

Vocabulary Building 3

Answer Key

A. 1. trade; **2.** producers; **3.** goods; **4.** consumers; **5.** exports; **6.** surplus

B. 1. intercontinental; **2.** Internet; **3.** interdependent; **4.** interchange; **5.** interpret; **6.** interviews

Teaching Notes

A. Completion: There are ten new vocabulary items highlighted on pages 132–133. Before attempting the definitions, ask students to use each term appropriately in a sentence for further practice. Then have the class complete the definitions in Activity A. Check answers as a class.

B. Word Link: The prefix *inter-* refers to things that happen between two or more people or things.

Students analyze the words in the box that start with the prefix and select them to complete the sentences in Activity B.

Challenge: Are you a producer, a consumer, or both? Explain your role in the economy. What do you produce that gets exported? What do you consume that is imported? Give specific examples.

Unit Introduction

This unit explores the effects of global warming on glaciers and on native people in the Arctic.

Key Words for Internet Research: *avalanche, carbon footprint, climate change, glacier melt, global warming, greenhouse gases (GHGs), Inuit hunter*

For More Information: http://environment.nationalgeographic.com/environment/global-warming/

Warm Up
Answer Key

1. Answers will vary. **2.** Glaciers and sea ice will melt, ocean levels will rise and flood coastal cities, more severe storms will occur, plants and animals will have difficulty coping with a warmer environment. **3.** People can reduce carbon emissions by using renewable types of energy.

Teaching Notes

Write the word *glacier* on the board and pronounce it [**glay** shur]. Tell students to look at the photo and read the caption. Ask them:

- **What is a glacier?** It is an extremely large mass of ice that moves very slowly, often down a mountain valley.
- **What are the things floating in the water?** They are pieces of the glacier that have broken off.
- **Where is the Grinnell Glacier?** In Glacier National Park in Montana, a state in northwest United States bordering Canada. See the location on the map on the next page.
- **What is special about this area?** It is part of the Waterton-Glacier International Peace Park, created with Canada as the world's first park between two countries in 1932. This important natural mountain ecosystem was recognized as a World Heritage Site in 1995.

Lesson 10A | A Warming World

Lesson Overview

Target Vocabulary:

consequences, critical, environmentalist, melt, shift, slide, solve, uncover, unexpected, unstoppable

Reading Passage Summary:

Read about the melting of glaciers in the Andes, Himalayan Mountains, and Greenland that may result in rising sea levels.

Answer Key

Before You Read

A. 1. Number 12, the Careser glacier in Italy; **2.** Number 8, the Nigardsbreen glacier in Norway; **3.** Norway
B. the Chacaltaya glacier in Bolivia and the Jacobshavn Isbræ glacier in Greenland

Reading Comprehension

A. 1. a; **2.** b (line 10); **3.** d (lines 36–38); **4.** c (line 39); **5.** d (lines 43–44)
B. 1. b; **2.** e; **3.** c; **4.** d; **5.** a; **6.** f

Vocabulary Practice

A. 1. critical; **2.** solve; **3.** Environmentalists; **4.** melts; **5.** unexpected
B. 1. slides; **2.** unstoppable; **3.** shifts; **4.** consequences; **5.** uncover

Teaching Notes

Before You Read

Have students look closely at the map and the charts. The map is a *polar projection*, from the perspective of looking down at the North Pole. The result is that the Northern Hemisphere is visible, but not the Southern. This is why the Chacaltaya glacier in Bolivia is not on the map. Draw attention to the key that shows glaciers in blue-green and ice shelves in white. Ask where these are found.

Then ask the class to comment about features of the chart on the right of page 136. Write the features on the board. They include a key at the top that shows years from 1977 to 2005, and the amount of change in thickness of the glaciers during this period. Thus, there are line graphs for each glacier listed. Compare the amount and angle of change between glaciers 4 (shallow change) and 12 (steep change). The numbers indicate the percentage of change. Although overall temperatures have warmed in recent decades, some places have experienced cooler temperatures and increased precipitation. An example might be the Nigardsbreen glacier in Norway.

A. Reading Charts: Have students work in pairs to answer the questions in Activity A. Check answers as a class.

B. Scan: Have students scan the reading passage for the names of the two glaciers in Activity B. Check answers as a class.

Reading Comprehension

A. Multiple Choice: Have students read the entire passage silently and answer the questions for Activity A. Check answers as a class, asking students to give evidence for their answers using line references from the reading passage.

B. Matching: Have students complete Activity B, and then check answers as a class. Have students volunteer to draw and explain cause-effect chains on the board.

Challenge: For students who have completed Activities A and B, write the following question on the board. Additional comprehension questions are available on the CD-ROM.

What message do the photos on pages 137–138 give?

Vocabulary Practice

A. Definitions: Have students do Activity A. Then, have students check answers with a partner.

B. Completion: Have students do Activity B. Check answers as a class.

Challenge: Ask students to find four pieces of information in the first vocabulary reading that environmentalists would probably disagree with.

At http://environment.nationalgeographic.com/environment/global-warming/extreme-ice-survey-article.html, students can watch time-lapse photography of a glacier actually melting.

Word Partnership

When you *uncover* something that is hidden or secret, you discover or find out about it. *When the security police uncovered the plot, they learned about the attack the terrorists had planned. Uncover* can also mean to physically take the cover off something. *The rescue dogs uncovered the skiers who were trapped by the sudden avalanche.*

Lesson Overview

Target Vocabulary:

access, corporation, ethnicity, fund, gun, quantity, resource, starving, sufficient, urgently

Reading Passage Summary:

Learn about the problems that Inuit hunters face as sea ice conditions change as a result of global warming.

Answer Key

Before You Read

A. 1. Greenland; **2.** walrus; **3.** winter; **4.** Qaanaaq (Thule)
B. by dogsled

Reading Comprehension

A. 1. b; **2.** b (line 27); **3.** c (lines 4–5, 14–16);
    4. d (paragraph 4); **5.** c (41–43)
B. 1. thick; **2.** access; **3.** the government; **4.** training;
    5. fishermen, power plants

Vocabulary Practice

A. 1. quantity; **2.** starving; **3.** access; **4.** resources;
    5. sufficient
B. 1. a; **2.** b; **3.** a; **4.** b; **5.** b

Teaching Notes

Before You Read

A. Discussion: The map shows detail of the area near Qaanaaq [pronounced kaah nack] in northwest Greenland. Have students locate the area on the globe. This location is also known as *Thule* [thew lee] and there is still an air force base nearby with that name. The red lines and arrows indicate the route the hunters take.

Students will read about Inuit [**in** new wit] hunters. The Inuit are the native people of the Arctic from Alaska across Canada to Greenland. These people were formerly known as *Eskimos*, but that term has a very negative meaning. Inuit means "the people" in their own Inuktitut language. For 1,500 years, the Inuit lived by fishing and hunting sea animals such as walrus, seals, and whales from the ice or in small boats called *kayaks*.

In 2007 National Geographic reported on an expedition to Baffin Island in the Canadian Arctic. The team, which included three Inuit hunters, traveled by dogsled. For reports on the project, see http://news.nationalgeographic.com/news/2007/05/070515-inuit-arctic.html.

B. Predict: Students use the map to predict how the hunters travel on the sea ice in Activity B. Note the key about ice thickness in winter. Also, have students refer back to the sea ice map on page 138. Check answers as a class.

Reading Comprehension

A. Multiple Choice: Have students read the entire passage silently and answer the questions for Activity A. Check answers as a class, asking students to give evidence for their answers using line references from the passage.

Question 2 asks for the best phrase to replace *at the same time*. Here, the purpose is to create contrast between traditional and modern ways of life, not to literally deal with time. Question 5 addresses a theme found throughout the reading passage. Although ice hunting is extremely difficult and dangerous, it represents a link with the past and a mark of ethnic group identity.

B. Completion: Remind students to limit their responses to two words. Have students complete Activity B, and then check answers as a class.

Challenge: For students who have completed Activities A and B, write the following question on the board. Additional comprehension questions are available on the CD-ROM.

Why do Inuit hunters use dogsleds instead of snowmobiles? Explain your answer.

Vocabulary Practice

A. Completion: Have students do Activity A. Then, have students check answers with a partner.

B. Words in Context: Have students do Activity B. Check answers as a class.

Challenge: For students who have completed Activities A and B, write the following questions on the board. Additional vocabulary questions are available on the CD-ROM.

1. How urgent is the problem of global warming for Arctic animals?

2. Do you think the Inuit hunters will have sufficient access to sea animal resources in coming years?

Explore More

Video Summary: The process, causes, and consequences of global warming are explained, as well as what we can do to stop it.

Answer Key

A. 1. atmosphere; **2.** ground; **3.** gases

B. 1. critical; **2.** quantity; **3.** sufficient; **4.** melt; **5.** consequences; **6.** unstoppable; **7.** solve; **8.** Environmentalists; **9.** urgently; **10.** resources

C. 1. Glaciers and sea ice will melt, ocean levels will rise and flood coastal cities, more severe storms will occur, plants and animals will have difficulty coping with a warmer environment. **2.** Answers will vary.

Teaching Notes

A. Preview: For suggestions on building students' viewing skills, see pages 19–20. Have students look at the diagram and read the caption. Have students complete Activity A and then check answers as a class. Brainstorm about what students know about the process of global warming.

If you have access to a computer in the classroom, visit a global warming interactive map at http://environment.nationalgeographic.com/environment/global-warming/gw-impacts-interactive.html.

This map summarizes most of the main points in the unit and introduces some other effects for students to think about. They include: species extinction, water shortages, severe storms, heat waves, reduced growing seasons, loss of biodiversity, and reduced forests.

B. Summarize: Follow these steps:
1. Have students watch the video through once, bearing in mind the answers they gave in the **Preview**.
2. Before playing the video a second time, ask students to read the summary and fill the gaps in Activity B with vocabulary items from the box. They close their books while watching the video.
3. After they've watched the video a second time, students complete or change their answers on the summary. Have them check answers with a partner.
4. If necessary, play the video through a third time and then check answers as a class.

C. Think About It: Have students answer the questions in Activity C in pairs. Discuss ideas as a class.

Unit 11 Incredible Insects

Unit Introduction

This unit describes the behavior of army ants and tells about detailed digital artwork that gives a new appreciation of the beauty of moths.

Key Words for Internet Research: *Abuku Sokoke Forest, army ants, butterfly farming, Eciton burchelli, Joseph Scheer, Lepidoptera, moths*

For More Information: http://animals.nationalgeographic.com/animals/bugs.html

Warm Up

Answer Key

1 and 2. Answers will vary. **3.** Answers will vary, but may include those with interesting life cycles such as butterflies and silkworms that go through *larva* (caterpillar) and *pupa* (cocoon) stages and then metamorphose into their winged adult state.

Teaching Notes

Tell students to look at the photo and read the caption. Ask them:
- **What is unusual about this butterfly?** Its wings are transparent like glass.
- **What is a cloud forest?** It's a tropical forest located in a place where there is constant moisture in the air in the form of cloud cover or fog. The moisture and warm environment result in heavy vegetation of mosses, ferns, and orchids that thrive in those conditions.

Insects are part of a group of animals called *arthropods* [**arth** row pods] that include spiders and centipedes. Unlike those arthropods, true insects have only six legs. Their three-part bodies consisting of a head, thorax, and abdomen have a rigid external covering, but no internal skeleton.

Some insects are pests that cause problems for people. For example, mosquitoes spread diseases like malaria and yellow fever, termites eat wooden houses, and locusts can wipe out crops. On the other hand, helpful insects pollinate plants, bees produce honey and wax, and silkworms produce silk.

Lesson 11A Small Wonders

Lesson Overview

Target Vocabulary:

blind, broaden, capability, constitute, cooperation, delay, fellow, loyalty, nest, observe

Reading Passage Summary:

Read about the highly coordinated social behavior of army ants.

Answer Key

Before You Read

A. from top to bottom, left to right: queen, major, submajor, media, minor

B. c. make a nest

Reading Comprehension

A. 1. c; **2.** a (lines 9–10); **3.** b; **4.** a; **5.** c

B. 1. 300,000; **2.** 320; **3.** 200,000; **4.** 300,000; **5.** 700,000

Vocabulary Practice

A. 1. nests; **2.** constitute; **3.** observed; **4.** fellow; **5.** loyalty

B. 1. a; **2.** a; **3.** b; **4.** a; **5.** b

Teaching Notes

Before You Read

Direct students' attention to the map showing the range of *Eciton burchelli* [**ess** it on birch **el** lee], a type of army ant. The ants described in the passage live in Panama, labeled on the map. Costa Rica, the location of the **Warm Up** photo, is the country just north of Panama.

A. Labeling: Have students work in pairs to match the labels with the pictures in Activity A. Direct them to the photo of ant jaws on page 150 as a helpful clue. Check answers as a class.

B. Predict: Students use the photo and caption on the bottom of 149 to answer the question in Activity B. Write the word *bivouac* [**biv** ooh wack] on the board and pronounce it. In the military, *bivouac* means a simple camp that is set up for an overnight stay. Ask how this contrasts with the ants' bivouac (see lines 18–23 in the passage). Check answers as a class.

Reading Comprehension

A. Multiple Choice: Have students read the entire passage silently and answer the questions for Activity A. Check answers as a class, asking students to give evidence for their answers using line references from the passage.

In Question 5, loyalty is an aspect of ant behavior, but "selfless cooperation" in line 46 implies that ants care for each other and work together.

B. Completion: Have students complete Activity B, and then check answers as a class.

Challenge: For students who have completed Activities A and B, write the following question on the board. Additional comprehension questions are available on the CD-ROM.

Give three examples of how army ants cooperate for the good of the group as a whole.

Vocabulary Practice

A. Completion: Have students do Activity A. Then, have students check answers with a partner.

B. Words in Context: Have students do Activity B. Check answers as a class.

Challenge: For students who have completed Activities A and B, write the following question on the board. Additional vocabulary questions are available on the CD-ROM.

Read the caption to the photo on page 152. Why do you think the ants' behavior causes problems for the plant species? (If the seed dries out, it won't sprout and fewer plants will live.)

Word Link

The prefix *co-* often means people doing things together, but not always. Ask students to use a dictionary to find words starting with *co-* that do have this meaning. Some suggestions in addition to those given in **Word Link** include *coalition*, *collaborate*, *collect*, and *coed*. Ask what they mean.

Unexpected Beauty

Lesson Overview

Target Vocabulary:

carelessly, congratulate, credit, darkness, declare, disturb, emerge, overwhelming, reaction, retain

Reading Passage Summary:

Artist Joseph Scheer uses digital scanning to produce extremely detailed images of moths collected from a friend's backyard.

Answer Key

Before You Read

A. 1. Photos 1. c; 2. a; 3. b; **2.** Answers will vary.
B. b. How moths were caught and images produced for an interesting display.

Reading Comprehension

A. 1. c (lines 5–6); **2.** d (lines 15–16); **3.** a (lines 36–37); **4.** a (line 40); **5.** b
B. 1. art; **2.** beauty; **3.** light; **4.** scanner; **5.** species

Vocabulary Practice

A. 1. retain; **2.** disturbed; **3.** reaction; **4.** darkness; **5.** emerge
B. 1. b; **2.** a; **3.** b; **4.** a; **5.** a

Teaching Notes

Before You Read

Have students look at all the photos and captions in Unit 11B. Use a **KWL** approach (**know**, **want** to find out, **learned**) for this topic. Ask the class to brainstorm what they know about these animals and write the information on the board. At the end of the unit after the video, revisit the list to see what has been learned.

A. Discussion: Have students work in small groups to make lists of characteristics of butterflies, moths, and dragonflies. Which of these things could they see in the photos? Some things like night-time activity and long migrations will not appear. Then have students do Activity A. Check answers as a class.

B. Skim for the Main Idea: Have students do Activity B. Check answers as a class.

Reading Comprehension

A. Multiple Choice: Have students read the entire passage silently and answer the questions for Activity A. Check answers as a class, asking

students to give evidence for their answers using line references from the passage.

B. Completion: Have students work in pairs. One student describes what Joseph Scheer and Mark Klingensmith did to collect the moths. The other student describes how Scheer made the images. Then the students work together to complete the summary using one word for each blank in Activity B. Check answers as a class.

Challenge: For students who have completed Activities A and B, write the following question on the board. Additional comprehension questions are available on the CD-ROM.

Do you think you would enjoy seeing the images of moths? Why or why not?

Vocabulary Practice

A. Completion: Have students do Activity A. Then, have students check answers with a partner.

B. Words in Context: Have students do Activity B. Check answers as a class.

Challenge: For students who have completed Activities A and B, write the following question on the board. Additional vocabulary questions are available on the CD-ROM.

Can you list four things moths and their caterpillars do to protect themselves from predators? (Hint: one answer is in the photo caption on page 157.)

Explore More

Video Summary: Watch how the Butterfly Project has helped the conservation of the Abuku Sokoke forest in Kenya and its hundreds of rare species of butterflies.

Answer Key

A. The animal is best shipped in the pupa stage because it is least active then and requires little care. Note: the plural of *pupa* is *pupae* [pronounced **poo pee**]. Write the word on the board.

B. 1. broadened; **2.** capable; **3.** darkness; **4.** emerge; **5.** cooperate; **6.** reaction; **7.** observe; **8.** retain; **9.** delay; **10.** declared

C. 1. Raising butterflies is a sustainable business that provides income to people without damaging the forest environment. **2.** It depends on how the butterflies are used. If they are released into the wild, they could compete with native butterflies and have a negative effect on their populations. Some butterfly farmers are careful to only ship butterflies that ordinarily live in that location. Other insects that are commercially traded include ladybugs that eat aphids that destroy greenhouse plants. The ladybugs provide a natural way to control the pests without using harmful chemicals. For more on the butterfly trade, visit http://butterflywebsite.com/ or http://www.naturekenya.org/Kipepeo.htm for specific information on the farm in Kenya.

Teaching Notes

A. Preview: For suggestions on building students' viewing skills, see pages 19–20. The video is about a commercial butterfly farm in Kenya. Ask students to tell about the stages of butterfly development.
- In the caterpillar or larva stage, the animal eats and grows a lot.
- During the pupa stage, the animal is enclosed within a cocoon and doesn't move very much. However, the pupa is undergoing *metamorphosis*.
- When the process is complete, a butterfly emerges.

Have students complete Activity A, thinking about which stage is best for shipment.

B. Summarize: Follow these steps:
  1. Have students watch the video through once, bearing in mind the answers they gave in the **Preview**.

  2. Before playing the video a second time, ask students to read the summary and fill the gaps in Activity B with vocabulary items from the box. They close their books while watching the video.
  3. After they've watched the video a second time, students complete or change their answers on the summary. Have them check answers with a partner.
  4. If necessary, play the video through a third time and then check answers as a class.

C. Think About It: Have students answer the questions in Activity C in pairs. Discuss ideas as a class.

Unit Introduction

This unit explores the extremes of private space flight and descent into the world's deepest cave.

Key Words for Internet Research: *Ansari X Prize, Burt Rutan, caving, Google Lunar X Prize, Krubera Cave, Oman caves, private space flight, SpaceShipOne, Virgin Galactic*

For More Information: http:// science.nationalgeographic.com/science/space/space-exploration/flying-high.html and http://ngm.nationalgeographic.com/ngm/0505/feature4/multimedia.html

Warm Up

Answer Key

Answers will vary (for all questions).

Teaching Notes

Tell students to look at the photo and read the caption. Ask them:

- **What is a test pilot?** A test pilot flies new aircraft to see if they really operate as they have been designed to fly. Being a test pilot is a very risky job as new planes can crash, causing pilots to die.
- **What does it take to be a test pilot?** First, you must be an exceptionally good pilot and knowledgeable about aircraft engineering and construction. Beyond that, you have to remain calm under pressure and be capable of solving problems as they occur.
- **What is a F/A-22?** This plane, also called a *Raptor* after birds like hawks, is a modern military fighter plane.
- **What is special about this plane?** It uses *stealth technology* which means that it is difficult to detect with enemy radar, infrared heat detectors, or any of the usual ways of knowing that an aircraft is operating. See http://www.kbvp.com/extreme-videos/f-22-raptor for a video of the F/A-22 in flight.

Lesson 12A | To the Edge of Space

Lesson Overview

Target Vocabulary:

aboard, crash, dozen, launch, license, requirement, resolve, scheme, thrill, weightless

Reading Passage Summary:

Read about the design, operation, and success of *SpaceShipOne*, the first private spaceship.

Answer Key

Before You Read

A. 1. Wright Flyer; **2.** Boeing 747; **3.** Space Shuttle *Columbia*; **4.** B-2 Spirit

B. *SpaceShipOne*, designed by Burt Rutan, the first private spacecraft

Reading Comprehension

A. 1. c; **2.** b (lines 5–7); **3.** c (lines 32–34); **4.** d (line 36); **5.** b (lines 40–42)

B. 1. NG; **2.** F; **3.** T; **4.** T

Vocabulary Practice

A. 1. launched; **2.** requirements; **3.** resolved; **4.** crashed; **5.** scheme

B. 1. a; **2.** a; **3.** b; **4.** a; **5.** a

Teaching Notes

Before You Read

Before starting the first activity, have students look closely at the illustration of aircraft on page 160. Have the class brainstorm types of aircraft shown in the photo, noting the distinctive features of each one. For example, early aircraft such as those used by the Wright brothers had double wings. Commercial aircraft before jets used propellers. The 747 has a unique "hump" on top unlike any other aircraft. Both the space shuttle and the modern stealth aircraft have characteristic special shapes.

A. Discussion: Have students work in pairs to answer the questions in Activity A. Students match the numbers of aircraft in the illustration with the numbers on the timeline. Check answers as a class.

B. Scan: Have students do Activity B. Check answers as a class.

Reading Comprehension

Until the 1980s, governments had a monopoly on spaceflights. The European Space Agency created the world's first commercial space transportation company with investors from ten European countries. Rutan's spaceship was the first manned private trip into space.

A. Multiple Choice: Have students read the entire passage silently and answer the questions for Activity A. Check answers as a class, asking students to give evidence for their answers using line references from the passage.

For Question 5, have students locate the places in the passage where the events are mentioned. They should look for time clues such as dates as well as for verb tenses. In the final paragraph, they will see that references to Virgin Galactic's space voyages are all in the future.

B. True or False: Have students complete Activity B, and then check answers as a class. Remind students that NG means that there is no information on the topic in the reading passage. Students who have looked ahead to page 164 may answer "F" for the first item because the pilot of *SpaceShipOne* is pictured there. However, there is no evidence for his role in the passage.

Challenge: For students who have completed Activities A and B, write the following question on the board. Additional comprehension questions are available on the CD-ROM.
1. What does *White Knight* do?
2. Why will *White Knight Two* be larger?

Vocabulary Practice

A. Completion: Have students do Activity A. Then, have students check answers with a partner.

The Ansari X Prize Foundation has created and publicized competitions to motivate people to make breakthroughs in fields that will benefit humanity. See the website at http://www.xprize.org/ for more information about these competitions.

B. Words in Context: Have students do Activity B. Check answers as a class.

Challenge: Compare and contrast *SpaceShipOne* with the plans for Virgin Galactic's first spaceship. Look at these features: size, weight requirements of passengers, number of pilots, and flight heights of the mother ships.

Usage

The noun *dozens* can be used in the plural as a subject to emphasize a large quantity when the exact number is not known. *Dozens of fans waited all night in the rain to buy concert tickets.*

Lesson Overview

Target Vocabulary:

dive, ease, exhilarated, necessity, option, relatively, rope, technique, tight, underground

Reading Passage Summary:

An international team explores the world's deepest cave and faces challenges as they descend.

Answer Key

Before You Read

A. 1. feat; 2. descent; 3. passage; 4. entrance
B. b. Game Over (lines 47–49)

Reading Comprehension

A. 1. d; 2. a (paragraph 3); 3. a (lines 30–32);
    4. d (line 36); 5. b (lines 35–36)
B. 1. e; 2. b; 3. c; 4. d; 5. a

Vocabulary Practice

A. 1. option; 2. eased; 3. rope; 4. relatively;
    5. necessity; 6. techniques; 7. dove; 8. underground;
    9. exhilarated
B. 1. ease; 2. underground; 3. Ropes; 4. option;
    5. Necessities; 6. technique; 7. dive; 8. exhilarated;
    9. relatively

Teaching Notes

Before You Read

The photos show three very different cave systems. Ask students what they see in each of the three photos. What else do they know about caves? In the bottom photo of the cave at Lascaux, prehistoric people painted pictures of animals on cave walls. Archeologists think that cave paintings were part of a religious ritual associated with hunting.

A. **Matching:** Have students use the bold words from the captions to match with the definitions in Activity A. Check answers as a class.

B. **Scan:** Have students do Activity B. Note that the *depths* refer to distance underground from the cave's entrance. The deepest point reached by the second team was 2,080 meters or 6,824 feet at a place called *Game Over*. Check answers as a class.

Reading Comprehension

The exploration of Krubera Cave included 56 cavers from seven different countries. Take time to explore the cave profile on page 167 with the class. The red start marker shows the *entrance* or *mouth* of the cave, as shown in the photo on the bottom of page 166. The "0" figures show that the cave's depth is measured from that point. Intermediate depth markers occur along the right side of the profile. The red finish label shows the final depth reached by the second team whose explorations are shown in yellow.

A. **Multiple Choice:** Have students read the entire passage silently and answer the questions for Activity A. Check answers as a class, asking students to give evidence for their answers using line references from the passage.

B. **Matching:** Using the depth measurements, students sequence events in the exploration in Activity B. Check answers as a class.

Challenge: For students who have completed Activities A and B, write the following question on the board. Additional comprehension questions are available on the CD-ROM.
1. Where is Khubera Cave located? In what country? (Georgia) What body of water is it near? (Black Sea) In what mountains is the cave found? (the Caucasus—line 10)
2. Cavers explored Krubera Cave before 2004. Using the profile on page 167, tell about when the previous expeditions occurred and what they found.

Vocabulary Practice

A. Completion: Have students do Activity A. Then, have students check answers with a partner.

B. Definitions: Have students do Activity B. Check answers as a class.

Challenge: For students who have completed Activities A and B, write the following question on the board. Additional vocabulary questions are available on the CD-ROM.

In which of these situations would you feel exhilarated? Why?

a. hearing men shoot guns **b.** finishing a successful climb **c.** discovering a new cave passage

Word Partnership

Ask the class to identify some *absolute necessities* for exploring caves. Possible answers are ropes, light sources (headlamps to keep hands free), helmets, wetsuits or other body covering, communication and first-aid equipment. For longer explorations, food, water, and tents are necessities.

Explore More

Video Summary: A group of Girl Scouts tests their confidence and teamwork by embarking on an unusual camping trip—exploring an underground cave.

Answer Key

A. 1. rapelling; **2.** caver; **3.** ledge; **4.** waterfall
B. 1. techniques; **2.** resolved; **3.** relatively; **4.** ropes; **5.** underground; **6.** tight; **7.** option; **8.** ease; **9.** confidence; **10.** exhilarating

C. 1. As Jessica indicates, the right attitude or mind-set is very important, as are caving techniques, an experienced guide, and physical fitness. **2.** Answers will vary.

Teaching Notes

A. Preview: For suggestions on building students' viewing skills, see pages 19–20. Have students look at the diagram and read the caption. Ask students to complete Activity A. Check answers as a class. Brainstorm about what students know about the techniques of caving. *Rappelling* [pronounced rah **pell** ing] means using a rope to descend into or ascend up out of a cave. The rope is securely attached to the top of the cave and also to a harness or vest that the caver wears.

B. Summarize: Follow these steps:
  1. Have students watch the video through once, bearing in mind the answers they gave in the **Preview**.

2. Before playing the video a second time, ask students to read the summary and fill the gaps in Activity B with vocabulary items from the box. They close their books while watching the video.

3. After they've watched the video a second time, students complete or change their answers on the summary. Have them check answers with a partner.

4. If necessary, play the video through a third time and then check answers as a class.

C. Think About It: Have students answer the questions in Activity C in pairs. Discuss ideas as a class.

Answer Key

A. Across: **1.** access; **3.** melt; **5.** disturb; **7.** launch; **10.** quantity; **12.** observe; **13.** critical; **15.** exhilarated; **16.** solve; **17.** scheme; **18.** nest; **19.** sufficient

Down: **2.** consequences; **4.** thrill; **6.** requirement; **8.** retain; **9.** declare; **11.** necessity; **12.** option; **14.** dozen

B. Arizona, five million, six million, Colorado River, 446 km, 1,829 m, glass pathway, raft, kayak, Hisatsinom/ Anasazi, 1,300, honeymooners

Teaching Notes

A. Crossword: Before students attempt the crossword in Activity A, have them review the vocabulary from Units 10 through 12 using the **Target Vocabulary** list on pages 177–178 where words are given with lesson numbers. Then, have students use the definitions to complete the crossword. They should fill in the words they know first, using letters as clues for more challenging items. Check answers as a class.

B. Notes Completion: Have students do Activity B. Check answers as a class.

World Heritage Spotlight: Grand Canyon National Park

Background Information

The Grand Canyon, so huge that it can be seen from space, is a steep valley formed by water erosion over millions of years. Other deep canyons include Yarlung Zangbo in Tibet, Cotahuasi Colca in Peru, and the Tekezé Gorge in Ethiopia. The largest known canyon in the solar system is on Mars, eroded when the planet had water. It is nine times the size of the Grand Canyon! Visit the site http://www.skyimagelab.com/marvalmar. html for photos of the Mars canyon.

The biggest mystery about the Grand Canyon is what happened to the Native American people who lived in the canyon around A.D. 1250. Archeological evidence and *petroglyphs*—rock pictures like those in the photo on page 173—show that people lived in the canyon for 10,000 years. The ancient people built mud or *adobe* homes in the cliff walls and had a successful culture until they suddenly left, leaving valuable belongings behind. Archeologists have theorized that the climate changed and a drought forced the ancient cliff dwellers to leave. Today's Pueblo Indians call the mysterious ancient people *Hisatsinom* [pronounced ee **sah** tse nom]

and believe they were ancestors. Students who want to pursue this mystery will also find information under the Navaho term *Anasazi*.

The first European to see the Grand Canyon was Spanish explorer García López de Cárdenas who arrived in 1540. However, the canyon wasn't explored scientifically until 1869 when John Wesley Powell traveled down the Colorado River.

The Hualapai Indians who live near the Grand Canyon today developed the Skywalk tourist attraction pictured on page 172. The project has been controversial because tribal leaders believe it disturbs sacred ground and environmentalists think it is not suitable for the canyon.

For More Information: Visit http://online.wr.usgs. gov/outreach/grandcanyon/index.html to view film footage of a Colarado River trip. Students can simulate running rapids on the Colorado River at http://www. pbs.org/wgbh/amex/canyon/sfeature/rapidintro. html. For a video of the skywalk, see http://www. nationalgeographic.com/grandcanyon/.

Teaching Notes

Overview: The text box on page 172 describes the formation of the Grand Canyon, its size today, and some of the options for visitors. Text boxes on page 173 discuss the native people associated with the Grand

Canyon and describe a mystery that happened in 1928. The background photo shows the depth of the canyon with the Colorado River at the base while other photographs highlight features and activities in the Grand Canyon. Other boxes provide information about the canyon as a World Heritage Site and a glossary for terms that appear in bold. Note that one of these—*spectacular*—appears in the caption for the main photo.

Teaching Suggestions: Give students time to explore the features of pages 172–173. Write the word *canyon* on the board and pronounce it [**can** yun]. Explain that it was originally a Spanish word, meaning large tube or pipe. Other words for this kind of structure are *valley*, *gorge*, *gully*, *chasm* [pronounced **caz** um], and *water gap*. Ask students about canyons or deep, narrow valleys in their countries. Some examples are Taroko Gorge in Taiwan and the Three Gorges area on the Yangtze River in China.

Photos, films, and postcards have made the Grand Canyon familiar to people all over the world. Some of the most famous views are the black-and-white photos by the renowned American photographer Ansel Adams. At http://www.archives.gov/research/ansel-adams/ students can see pictures of the Grand Canyon as well as topics covered earlier in the book such as glaciers

and caves. Meanwhile, ask students what they already know about Grand Canyon and list information on the board. After they have read the spread, ask what new information they learned. Then have students work in groups of four to plan a trip to the Grand Canyon. Here are some things they will want to consider:

- Where is the Grand Canyon? How do they get there?
- What is the main reason for their visit?
- What are some of the ways to explore the Grand Canyon? Are some riskier than others? Why?
- Would they like to walk on the Skywalk? What could they see from it?
- What native people still live near the canyon?
- What records of ancient people exist there?

When each group has come up with an itinerary for their visit, have them explain it to another group.

Challenge: In the other three reviews featuring World Heritage Sites, which is most like the Grand Canyon and why? (The Great Barrier Reef in Australia is also a *natural* site, while the others are *cultural* and man-made.)

A Global View: Climate

Background Knowledge

To prepare students for the topic, ask some of the following questions:

- What is the difference between *climate* and *weather*? (*Climate* refers to long-term patterns and averages while *weather* refers to day-to-day changes in the atmosphere.]
- How would you describe the climate for your home country?

- Does that place have *seasons* at different times of year? Explain.
- What are some of the factors that affect climate? (latitude, elevation, position on a continent)
- Do you think climates are changing? If so, how and why?
- What do you think is an ideal climate? Where could you find this climate?

Teaching Notes

Overview: Pages 174–175 deal with the general topic of climate, climate zones, the relationship between climate and seasons, and the warming earth. These topics are illustrated with two world maps and a diagram.

Key Words for Internet Research: *climate, climate zones, droughts, heat waves, seasons, weather*

For More Information: See http://science. nationalgeographic.com/science/earth/earths-atmosphere/climate-article.html for more information about influences on climate and climate groups. The

video at http://video.nationalgeographic.com/video/ player/science/earth-sci/climate-weather-sci.html helps distinguish between climate and weather with graphic examples.

Building Visual Literacy

Map Reading: Climate Zones (bottom, page 174)

The map on page 174 shows major climate zones in the world. Some place names and geographic features are shown. The color key for the map is to the right on page 175. The beige text box on the right talks about major climate categories that get further developed in the key. They are:

- **Tropical climates** in the zone between the Tropic of Capricorn south of the Equator to the Tropic of Cancer north of the Equator. In this region the amount of sunlight is fairly constant throughout the year and there is less seasonal change. Within the tropics, some areas are wet because of frequent rainfall while others are dry.
- **Mild climates** occur where factors such as ocean currents and winds result in temperatures that are not extremely cold in winter nor extremely warm in summer. Examples are the Mediterranean and the California coast.
- **Continental climates** are at higher latitudes further from the Equator. They have distinct seasons featuring hot summers and cold winters.
- **Polar climates** exist at the extremes away from the Equator. Summers are cool with extremely long days and winters are frigid with many days without any sunlight at all.

Note that some climates are intermediate between the main categories. For example, *subarctic*, found in Canada and Siberia, is a combination of continental and polar.

Ask what climates the colors refer to and find examples of each color. Draw attention to the factors listed in paragraph 2 on page 174. Mountain ranges at high elevations can have very different climates than places at the same latitude. Ocean currents, such as the warm Gulf Stream, influence the European climate and make it much milder than it would be otherwise. Refer back to the map on pages 90–91 for warm and cold ocean currents.

Map Reading: The Warming Earth

The world map on pages 174–175 is color-coded to show changes in surface temperatures over a 30-year period from 1976 to 2006. The key on page 175 is for Celsius on the top and Fahrenheit on the bottom. Blue colors show places that have cooled while red tones are used for places that have warmed. Note that this map has outlines of land areas and indicates changes in the temperature of surface waters of the oceans. Only continents are marked on the map.

Ask about the parts of earth that have experienced the most change for warming and cooling. Ask students the following questions to check comprehension:

- **What area has been most severely affected by warming?** The Arctic
- **Of the areas which have become warmer, which have high population densities?** Europe, North America, China
- **Which have low populations densities?** The Arctic and Antarctic, Siberia
- **What are some consequences of global warming?** Rising sea levels will be a threat to low-lying coastal lands

Reading Diagrams

The diagram on the top of page 175 shows how the *tilt* of Earth on its axis as it rotates around the Sun creates seasons of hot and cold. Remind the class that seasons in the Northern and Southern hemispheres are opposite. Ask students the following questions to check comprehension:

- Which are the winter months in Sydney and New York City?
- Can there be other seasonal differences other than temperature? (Yes, in many places there are wet and rainy seasons. In India, for example, the yearly monsoon creates a rainy season.)

Vocabulary in Context

Some new vocabulary is defined in parentheses or by the surrounding words. Ask the class about the meaning of the following words: *latitude*, *proximity*, *drought*, *zones*, *solar energy*, and *elevation*.

Word Link

The suffix *-ologist* means "someone who studies something". What do these root words mean: *bio*, *geo*, *socio*, *psych*, and *zoo*? (life, earth, groups of people, the mind, and animals)

Critical Thinking

Have students answer the question: What, if anything, can be done to prevent the negative consequences of climate change?

Vocabulary Building 4

Answer Key

A. hemisphere; latitude; zone; summer; heat wave; climatologists; drought

B. 1. zoologist; **2.** archeologist; **3.** climatologist; **4.** psychologist; **5.** geologist; **6.** meteorologist; **7.** sociologist; **8.** paleontologist

Teaching Notes

A. Completion: Have students do Activity A. Check answers as a class.

B. Word Link: Students have additional practice with the suffix -*ologist* as they match profession names with work. As a review, have students look through units in the student book that feature these professions. For example, *biologists* feature in Units 2, 6, and 11, *archeologists* in Unit 3 and Review 1, and *meteorologists* in Unit 5.

Challenge: How can a temperature rise of 4°C create such problems in Europe? (People, plants, animals, and buildings are not prepared for such an increase.)

Name: _____ Class: _____

Reading Explorer: Reading Summary

Unit: _____ Reading title: _____

A. What is the reading passage mostly about?

_____

B. What places are mentioned in the reading?

_____

_____

C. In a few words, give the topic or main idea of each paragraph:

1. _____

2. _____

3. _____

4. _____

5. _____

6. _____

7. _____

D. Describe one of the photos or graphics in the reading. Did it give you an example of something in the text or provide additional information? Explain.

_____

_____

E. List the ten words highlighted in the text. Write a sentence or definition for each.

1. _____ _____

2. _____ _____

3. _____ _____

4. _____ _____

5. _____ _____

6. _____ _____

7. _____ _____

8. _____ _____

9. _____ _____

10. _____ _____

F. Make a sentence using one of the words in the footnotes.

_____

G. What are two or three things that you learned from this reading?

_____

_____

Name: _____ Class: _____

Reading Explorer: Video Worksheet

Unit: _____ Video title: _____

A. While viewing: Note the people, locations, and events that you see in the video.

_____

_____

_____

_____

B. After viewing: In a few words, give the main idea of the video.

_____

_____

C. Answer these questions about the video:

Where was it filmed? Give the name of the location(s) and continent(s):

_____

Who are the people in the video (if any)? What are their jobs?

_____

_____

What was the main *purpose* of the video? For example, to give information, to entertain, or to persuade you to change your mind about something.

_____

_____

D. Were there words or phrases in the video that were new to you? Note them here, with a definition or sample sentence.

_____

_____

_____

E. What are two or three things that you learned from the video?

_____

_____

_____

F. If *you* could film this video, what would you do differently?

_____

_____

Video Worksheet   **87**

Name: _____ Class: _____

Reading Explorer: World Heritage Spotlight Worksheet

Check the type of site: ☐ cultural ☐ natural ☐ both

A. Where is the site? _____ _____ _____
                                         place name   country   continent

B. When did it become a UNESCO World Heritage Site? _____

C. Why is this site important? Give two or more reasons:

_____

_____

_____

_____

_____

D. Were there words or phrases in the *World Heritage Spotlight* that were new to you? Note them here, with a definition or sample sentence.

_____

_____

_____

_____

E. Make a sentence using one of the words in the Glossary.

_____

_____

F. What are two or three aspects of the site that interest you the most?

   1. _____

   2. _____

   3. _____

G. Are there similar sites in or near your own country? In what way are they similar?

_____

_____

_____

_____

Reading Explorer: Global View Worksheet

A. What is the main topic of this Global View? _____

B. What are the key ideas described in the main text (see yellow column on left page)?

   1. _____

   2. _____

   3. _____

C. Choose one of the graphics in this Global View. Describe what it shows.

_____

_____

_____

D. List the words highlighted in color, with a sentence or definition.

_____

_____

_____

_____

E. How does this global issue relate to *your* life and where *you* live? The **Critical Thinking** question may help you.

_____

_____

_____

F. Draw a concept map to summarize the ideas in this Global View.

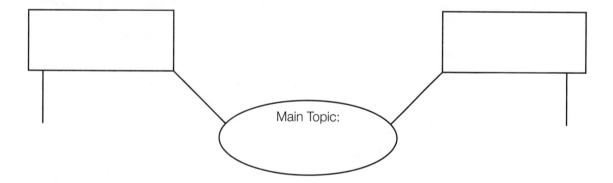

Main Topic:

Target Vocabulary Definitions

Word	Definition
aboard	(prep.) on a ship or plane
access	(n.) a way or right to reach or enter a place
account (for)	(v. phrase) to be responsible for or to explain
accurate	(adj.) correct to a very detailed level
acquire	(v.) to get or obtain something
administration	(n.) the management and supervision of an organization
admire	(v.) to like or respect someone or something
alarm	(v.) to make someone afraid that something dangerous might happen
analyze	(v.) to carefully examine something in order to fully understand it
appeal	(v.) to attract or be interesting to someone
approximate	(adj.) close to correct but not exact, estimated
arrange	(v.) to organize in order or in a particular position
aspect	(n.) part of something's character or nature
associate (with)	(v.) to connect with something else
assume	(v.) to suppose that something is true
attach (to)	(v.) to join or fasten something to something else
attack	(v.) to hurt or damage someone or something with physical violence
authority	(n.) an expert or someone who knows a lot about a subject
aware	(adj.) conscious that something is present or happening
base	(n.) the main or lowest part of something, the starting place
beneath	(prep.) under something
bite	(v.) to use teeth to cut into or through something
blame	(v.) to believe or say that someone or something is responsible for something bad
blind	(adj.) unable to see
brilliant	(adj.) extremely bright
broaden	(v.) to become wider
budget	(n.) an amount of money available to spend

Word	Definition
camp	(n.) a place where people live in tents
capability	(n.) the ability or power to do something
careless	(adj.) not paying attention to what one is doing, reckless
categorize	(v.) to decide which group or category things belong to
cave	(n.) a large hole in the side of a hill or underground
ceiling	(n.) the top inside surface of a room
ceremony	(n.) a formal event with special rituals or actions
circumstance	(n.) a condition that affects what happens in a particular situation
civilization	(n.) a human society with its own social organization and culture
claim	(v.) to say that something is true that is not proven
combination	(n.) a mixture of things
commercial	(n.) an advertisement broadcast on radio or television
complex	(adj.) complicated with many different parts, difficult to understand
comprehend	(v.) to understand
conduct	(v.) to organize and carry out an activity or task
confusion	(n.) a situation in which everything is in disorder and unclear
congratulate	(v.) to express pleasure about something good that has happened
consent	(v.) to give permission for someone to do something
consequence	(n.) the result of doing something
conservation	(n.) saving and protecting the environment
considerable	(adj.) great in amount or degree, a lot
constant	(adj.) happening all the time, continuous
constitute	(v.) to make up, to compose something that has parts or members
consume	(v.) to eat or drink, or to use something
contrast	(n.) a difference between two or more things
contribute	(v.) to say or do something positive and helpful

convenient	(adj.) easy, useful, and suitable for a particular purpose
cooperate	(v.) to work together with other people toward a common goal
corporation	(n.) a large business or company
crash	(v.) to smash against something violently, to fail
creature	(n.) any living thing that is not a plant
credit	(v.) to attribute good qualities to some other source
critical	(adj.) extremely important or urgent
cruel	(adj.) mean, deliberately causing pain or distress
cultural	(adj.) related to the arts, ideas, or customs of a society
curious	(adj.) interested in knowing and learning about things
current	(adj.) happening at the present time
cycle	(n.) a series of events or processes that are repeated again and again
darkness	(n.) nighttime, a condition without light
debatable	(adj.) not certain, questionable, doubtful
declare	(v.) to formally or officially state that something is true
deduce	(v.) to reach a conclusion because of other things you know to be true, to reason from general to specific
delay	(v.) to slow or stop for a time
demonstrate	(v.) to make something clear, to show
derive	(v.) to get or obtain
dimension	(n.) a measurement or size
display	(v.) to show or put something in a place where people can see it
distinct	(adj.) different from other things of the same type
distribute	(v.) to give or hand out something to a number of people
disturb	(v.) to interrupt, upset, or bother someone
dive	(v.) to go under the surface of the water using special breathing equipment
domestic	(adj.) referring to animals that are not wild but are kept on a farm or as pets
dominate	(v.) to be the most powerful or important person or thing in a situation
dozen	(num.) twelve of something

ease	(v.) to move slowly, carefully, and gently
economic	(adj.) related to money and resources
emerge	(v.) to come out of a place where one could not be seen
emphasis	(n.) the focus or special importance given to an activity or thing
employment	(n.) a job paying a salary or wages
enable	(v.) to make something possible
enemy	(n.) someone who intends to harm you because they hate you
energize	(v.) to fill with energy, to provide power
engineer	(n.) a person highly trained in science and mathematics who designs and builds machines, roads, and bridges
environmentalist	(n.) a person who is concerned with protecting and preserving the natural environment
essence	(n.) a basic and most important characteristic of something that gives it its individual identity
establish	(v.) to create or develop something
ethnicity	(n.) the identification with a particular cultural group such as race, country of origin, or religion
evidence	(n.) words or objects that support the truth of something, proof
exclude	(v.) to keep out or leave out
exhilarated	(adj.) a state of happiness or excitement
export	(v.) to send something out of the country to be sold
expose	(v.) to uncover something so it can be seen
factual	(adj.) true, based on facts
feature	(v.) to highlight something important
fellow	(adj.) beings with whom one has something in common
finance	(v.) to provide money to pay for a project or purpose
focus	(n.) the thing people concentrate on or pay most attention to
forecast	(n.) a statement about what is expected to happen in the future, especially in regard to weather
freeze	(v.) to change a liquid into a solid state due to low temperature
fund	(v.) to provide money for a person, program, or organization

garbage	(n.) waste material, especially from a kitchen	jealous	(adj.) envious, wanting something or someone belonging to another person
gather	(v.) to collect	jewelry	(n.) objects, usually made of precious metal, which are worn on the body, such as rings, necklaces, and bracelets
generation	(n.) a group of people of approximately the same age, or the period of time that it takes for children to grow up and become adults		
government	(n.) the group of people responsible for running a country	journal	(n.) a written record such as a diary or notebook
grip	(v.) to hold something firmly with your hand	joy	(n.) a feeling of great happiness
guard	(v.) to watch and protect people or things	labor	(n.) hard, physical work
		launch	(v.) to send a rocket, missile, or spacecraft into space
gun	(n.) a weapon from which bullets are fired	layer	(n.) one thickness that covers a surface between other levels
handle	(v.) to deal with or take care of,	license	(n.) an official permit to do, use, or own something
harm	(v.) to injure or damage someone or something	liquid	(n.) a substance that is neither solid nor gas but a fluid that can be poured
hero	(n.) someone who has done something brave, new, or good and who is admired by a lot of people	locate	(v.) to put in a particular place
		loyalty	(n.) the quality of staying firm in your friendship or support of someone or something
horror	(n.) a feeling of shock, fear, and worry caused by something extremely unpleasant		
humid	(adj.) an atmosphere of damp air or weather	luggage	(n.) suitcases and bags that people take when they travel
hypothesize	(v.) to use a working theory based on an unproved assumption	luxurious	(adj.) very comfortable and expensive
		melt	(v.) to change from a solid to a liquid because it has been heated
ignore	(v.) to pay no attention to someone or something	mineral	(n.) a substance such as tin, salt, or sulfur that is formed naturally in the Earth
illustrate	(v.) to make a point or situation clearer		
immigration	(n.) the process of people coming into a country to live or work	misfortune	(n.) something unpleasant or unlucky
impact	(v.) to create a forceful contact or blow	modernize	(v.) to change something by replacing old equipment or methods with new ones
imply	(v.) to indicate or suggest indirectly	murder	(v.) to kill someone
import	(v.) to bring products into one country from another	nearby	(adv.) only a short distance away
infection	(n.) a disease or sickness	necessity	(n.) something essential for life such as water or air
initial	(adj.) the first, something that happens at the beginning of a process	negative	(adj.) unpleasant, depressing, or harmful
injury	(n.) damage done to a person or animal's body	nest	(n.) a place where birds or other animals raise their young
interact	(v.) to communicate with others through conversation, looks, or actions	obedient	(adj.) willing to follow or obey rules or orders
international	(adj.) having to do with two or more nations	object	(v.) to be against something
		objective	(adj.) something one is trying to achieve
invade	(v.) to enter by force without permission	observe	(v.) to watch closely and carefully

obtain	(v.) to get or acquire
occasionally	(adv.) once in a while, infrequently
option	(n.) a choice, an alternative
origin	(n.) the location where something began, the source
overwhelming	(adj.) affecting one so strongly that one cannot deal with it
palace	(n.) a large, impressive house, the official home of a king, queen, or ruler
partnership	(n.) a relationship in which two or more people or groups work together
perceive	(v.) to see, notice, or realize something
permit	(v.) to allow one to do something
plenty	(adj.) a large quantity of something, more than is needed
policy	(n.) a government rule or strategy for doing something
pollute	(v.) to contaminate, to make dangerous or dirty
predictable	(adj.) obvious in advance what will happen
preserve	(v.) to take action to save or protect something, or keep it in its original state
prevent	(v.) to ensure that something does not happen
prior	(adj.) earlier, previous
process	(n.) a series of actions or events that have a particular result
professional	(adj.) relating to a person's work, especially work that requires special training or qualifications
profitable	(adj.) bringing in more money than is spent
purchase	(v.) to buy something
pure	(adj.) clean, not dirty or polluted; not mixed with other things
qualify	(v.) to have the right to do or have something, or to be called something
quantity	(n.) an amount
reaction	(n.) a response, what you feel, say, or do after an experience
relatively	(adv.) comparatively with regard to size or quality
remarkable	(adj.) outstanding, extraordinary, worthy of attention
remote	(adj.) distant, referring to a far-away place or time
renowned	(adj.) famous, well known

require	(v.) to need (something)
reserve	(v.) to keep something for a special purpose, to set aside
reside	(v.) to live (in a certain place)
resolve	(v.) to make a firm decision to do something
resource	(n.) something useful and valuable like money or materials
restrict	(v.) to put a limit on something
retain	(v.) to keep
reunite	(v.) to bring people together again after they have been separated
rope	(n.) a thick cord or wire that is made by twisting together several smaller cords or wires
rotate	(v.) to turn
scheme	(n.) a plan for achieving something that will be of benefit
sector	(n.) a division or part of something, especially government
selection	(n.) a choice
shallow	(adj.) not deep
shame	(n.) an uncomfortable feeling when one has done something wrong
shift	(n.) a change in position or location
sightsee	(v.) to travel around visiting places of interest
sink	(v.) to move slowly downward or disappear below the surface of water
slide	(v.) to move easily and quietly across a surface
solve	(v.) to find an answer or solution to a problem
source	(n.) a place where one gets or obtains something
starve	(v.) to suffer greatly from lack of food
sufficient	(adj.) enough of something
supposedly	(adv.) as it seems or is assumed
surround	(v.) to circle all around
symbol	(n.) a sign, shape, or object that represents something else that is important or meaningful in a culture
talent	(n.) a natural ability to do something well
technique	(n.) a particular method of doing an activity

teenager (*n.*) a young person between the ages of thirteen and nineteen

tent (*n.*) a shelter made of cloth often used by people who are camping

theory (*n.*) a possible explanation for something that has yet to be confirmed

threaten (*v.*) to say or imply that you will hurt someone

thrill (*n.*) a feeling of strong excitement or pleasure

tight (*adj.*) holding or fitting closely without extra space

tiny (*adj.*) extremely small

trade (*n.*) a type of business or commerce

translator (*n.*) a person who interprets from one language to another

uncover (*v.*) to be without a cover, to remove a cover

underground (*adj.*) below the surface of the ground

undertake (*v.*) to start doing a task and take responsibility for it

unexpected (*adj.*) surprising because you did not think something would happen

unknown (*adj.*) not known

unparalleled (*adj.*) extraordinary, something without an equal

unstoppable (*adj.*) impossible to stop

upward (*adv.*) rising, going up

urgent (*adj.*) demanding immediate attention

variety (*n.*) different types of things

voyage (*n.*) a long journey in a ship or on a spacecraft

wealth (*n.*) possession of a large amount of money or valuable things

wedding (*n.*) a marriage ceremony and the party after it

weightless (*adj.*) without weight, as in space

widespread (*adj.*) spread or existing over a large area

wisdom (*n.*) the ability to use experience and knowledge in making sensible decisions

wrap (*v.*) to fold cloth or paper tightly around something to cover it

Glossary of Terms

Term	Definition
affix	letters added to the beginning (prefix) or end (suffix) of a word that change the word's meaning and part of speech
caption	a title or description printed underneath or next to a photograph or other graphic
chunking	reading text in groups of words such as phrases, not reading word by word
cloze	a technique for checking comprehension of a text by omitting words from a passage and substituting gaps
collocation	words that frequently occur together, for example, "blonde hair"
extensive reading	reading longer texts outside the classroom, primarily for interest or pleasure, at a language level that is appropriate for the reader
gist comprehension	understanding the general meaning or sense of a text
graphic organizer	a visual way of showing the relationship of ideas from a text. Examples used in *Reading Explorer* are timelines, Venn diagrams, and word webs.
high-frequency vocabulary	the most commonly occurring and useful words that students need to know for reading
inference	understanding meaning that is not directly stated in a text; "reading between the lines"
intensive reading	guided, detailed reading often done in class for a particular purpose, such as building vocabulary or developing reading skills
linear text	prose or written text, as contrasted to graphically presented material such as photographs, videos, maps, and charts
main idea	the most important idea of a paragraph or entire reading passage
mnemonic	a memory aid, such as associating a word with a picture, to make something easier to learn or remember
paraphrasing	expressing the same idea using different words
reference	the relationship between a word—for example, a pronoun such as *it* and *him*—which stands for another name, word, or idea mentioned elsewhere in the reading passage
scan	to read quickly in search of specific information, such as names and dates
skim	to read quickly to determine the gist of a passage or the main ideas
subvocalizing	pronouncing words quietly while reading; moving lips, tongue, and throat
summary	a short account of a reading or video that gives only the main ideas
timeline	a graphic organizer that shows the relationship between events in chronological order. For example, see page 16 of this Teacher's Guide.
Venn diagram	a type of graphic organizer with two or more overlapping circles that indicate comparison (where things are the same) and contrast (where things are different). For example, see page 16 of this Teacher's Guide.
visual literacy	understanding and interpreting information in the form of photographs, videos, maps, and graphic images such as charts and diagrams; also referred to as "graphic literacy."
word map	a graphic organizer that shows how words and ideas are related to each other

Recommended Graded Readers

The *Footprint Reading Library* is a nonfiction series of graded readers that presents fascinating real-life stories in three formats: print, audio, and video. The series uses material from National Geographic Digital Media and is an ideal accompaniment to *Reading Explorer*, particularly for after-class extensive reading practice.

Each of the units in *Reading Explorer 2* is tied—thematically and in terms of approximate language level—with one of the *Footprint Reading Library* titles; see the following table.

For more information on the *Footprint Reading Library*, visit elt.heinle.com/ng

Unit	Theme	Recommended Footprint title
1	On the Menu	Solar Cooking*
2	Animals and Language	Orangutan Language*
3	History Detectives	The Lost Temples of the Maya*
Review 1	Buried Cities	Living with a Volcano
4	Great Destinations	Gliding Across the Gobi*
5	Storms	Wind Power
6	Reef Encounters	Cupid the Dolphin*
Review 2	Underwater Wonders	Dangerous Dining
7	Sweet Scents	Birds in Paradise
8	Great Explorers	The Art of Making Silk*
9	Traditions and Rituals	The Olympians*
Review 3	Cities of Gold and Mud	One Boy's Journey
10	Global Warming	The Missing Snows of Kilimanjaro
11	Incredible Insects	Killer Bees!
12	Going to Extremes	The Adventure Capital of the World
Review 4	The Grand Canyon	The Three Rivers of Zambia*
Titles marked * are at 1,600 headwords level; other titles are at 1,300 headwords level.		